MW00912771

TAPPING
YOUR

# Inner Strength

## How to Find the

## Resilience to

## Deal with

## Anything

EDITH HENDERSON GROTBERG, Ph.D.

New Harbinger Publications, Inc.

*This book is dedicated to all those courageous people who showed us how to overcome the adversities of life. They suffered; they conquered; they were transformed; they were resilient.*

## Publisher's Note

Distributed in the U.S.A. by Publishers Group West; in Canada by Raincoast Books; in Great Britain by Airlift Book Company, Ltd.; in South Africa by Real Books, Ltd.; in Australia by Boobook; and in New Zealand by Tandem Press.

Copyright © 1999 by Edith Henderson Grotberg, Ph.D.
New Harbinger Publications, Inc.
5674 Shattuck Avenue
Oakland, CA 94609

Cover design by SHELBY DESIGNS & ILLUSTRATES
Edited by Donna Long
Text design by Tracy Marie Powell

Library of Congress Catalog Card Number: 99-74371
ISBN 1-57224-168-3 Paperback

Printed in Canada.

New Harbinger Publications' Website address: www.newharbinger.com

01   00   99
10   9   8   7   6   5   4   3   2   1
First printing

# Contents

# Acknowledgments

We are, indeed, a world bonded by common experiences of adversity. All of us experience death of loved ones, loss of jobs, rejection by friends, and battered self-confidence. Many of us experience fires, earthquakes, wars, floods, and hurricanes. Each of these adversities challenges our ability to deal with them, to overcome them, to learn from them, and to be transformed by them.

My mission in life during the past years has been to learn how people deal with these adversities, especially how they acquire the ability to deal with them. The most effective means is resilience. This fact became clear to me as a result of gathering research data from twenty-seven sites in twenty-two countries around the world. So, my acknowledgments begin with those wonderful people at the different sites who gladly conducted the research to determine how adults apply resilience to their own lives and how they promote resilience in their children. This book would not exist without their work. Nor would it exist without the support of the Civitan International Research Center, University of Alabama at Birmingham.

Further acknowledgment goes to the Bernard van Lee Foundation, where my 1995 book, *A Guide for Promoting Resilience in Children,* was published and distributed worldwide, free of charge. The Foundation, with the leadership of Jorge Laffitte, also supported the development of the website: **resilnet@uiuc.edu**. Thanks also to Donna Long for her careful attention to detail and focus on clarity of messages.

I joyfully acknowledge all those who told me their personal experiences of adversity during the many workshops I conducted on resilience, and those who shared their experiences with the public through talk shows, newspaper features, and public presentations. They are role models for dealing with adversities.

My husband, Dr. Lee Burchinal, is a sociologist and information specialist. He gives me a larger perspective than the psychologist's focus on the individual. And when I have trouble with the computer and its many permutations, I have a fail-proof solution: "LEE!"

# Introduction

Just one day, one issue, one newspaper (*Washington Post*, 11 August 1998): there are three articles that give examples of drawing on resilience to overcome the inevitable adversities of life.

In an article titled "Private Loss, Public Battle: Family of Slain Fairfax Teen Puts Grief to Work for Others," staff writer Brooke A. Masters describes the following example of resilience:

A mother, responding to the death of her daughter who was shot in a road-rage incident, stated, "You hurt so much on the inside that you don't know if it's physical or emotional. I think it's going to take a lifetime." However, drawing on her resilience to deal with this tragedy, she and her family eventually decided to form Ann's Campaign. They display and distribute cards that read, Smile More, Care More, Love More, Be More Understanding. They have also set up a website address for interactions and information. The mother explains, "People die, but love doesn't, and that love is a driving force to try and make this a better and safer America."

In an article on needle risk, writer Kathleen F. Phalen shows that while hundreds of medical workers become infected with the AIDS or hepatitis viruses from accidental punctures each year, some of those people are still able to demonstrate resilience:

"The patient suddenly moved.... It was violent and he hit my hand, the one that held the needle. It punctured my latex glove and was thrust into my left palm." This statement by a recently graduated critical-care nurse describes the incident that began her experience of adversity, with dire consequences. She later learned that the patient had AIDS, and six months later she tested positive for HIV. "As soon as I walked in the door of the employee health office, I knew. I looked at the nurse and she had tears in her eyes, and I started crying. It was all over." However, drawing on her resilience to deal with this tragedy, she soon decided to join a battle for safer devices in all hospitals to protect against the transmission of infectious diseases by needles. "The people I worked with always made fun of me because I always got my goggles, wore my gloves. That's the irony of it." She had taken both steps when she was stuck. But, in addition to her joining the national battle for new legislation, she continued to spend a great deal of her time trying to educate workers about the hazards.

Writer Stephen Washington describes the following tale in an article entitled, "After the Explosion, Silence: A Survivor's 36 Hours with the Missing and the Dead":

A forty-eight-year-old man, trapped for thirty-six hours in a tiny space as a result of the American-embassy bombing in Nairobi, Kenya, drew on his resilience from the beginning. Realizing he was trapped and had multiple injuries, he struck a match and saw he had fallen into a pocket in the rubble. He took off his belt and used it to pull himself closer to the staircase, as protection against more falling debris. Then he waited and prayed. He thought about death and about whether another explosion would come. He tried not to think about time. As he was being rescued, he assured a woman trapped nearby that she would be rescued, too. Later he said he knew his own courage and presence of mind had combined with the skills of the rescue team to save his life. "The courage of the mind is greater than . . . the body. I never gave up hope."

# Resilience and the Adversities of Life

Life is full of experiences of adversity. Some of them are external, such as fires, earthquakes, floods, drought, bombings, wars, or violence. Some of them are within the family, such as divorce, abuse, abandonment, or loss of a job, home, or loved one. And some of them are within the individual, such as fear of rejection, loss of love, harm, failure, or illness.

However, there are differences in what is perceived as an adversity, particularly in personal experiences. One person may perceive a divorce as an adversity, while another may perceive it as the only way to be safe from harm. One person may see the loss of a job as an adversity, while another may see it as an opportunity to be free to pursue more education or another, less stressful job. But when anyone has an experience that causes great stress, fear, a sense of vulnerability, or alienation, that person may well perceive the experience to be an adversity. Resilience is the human capacity to face, overcome, be strengthened by, and even be transformed by experiences of adversity.

Resilience is not magic; it is not found only in certain people and it is not a gift from unknown sources. All humans have the capacity to become resilient—everyone is able to learn how to face the inevitable adversities of life; everyone is able to overcome adversities and be strengthened by them. And everyone can be transformed by these experiences. Obviously there are many individual differences, depending on such things as age, stage of development, the number and frequency of the adversities, and the resources available to deal with them. But you can begin or enhance the process at any age or stage of your life.

Where are you today in terms of being resilient? Here is an exercise to help you find out. As you read this book and do the exercises in later chapters, you will come back to this exercise to see if there are changes in your resilience quotient.

# What Is Your Resilience Quotient Today?

Read each of the following statements, and think about how much each one describes you. Then write down a number from 1 to 10, with 10 representing "describes me the most." Then add the score numbers for all twenty-one statements: that total is your resilience quotient today.

Resilience on _____ (fill in the date) = _____

### I Have

1. One or more persons within my family I can trust and who love me without reservation.

2. One or more persons outside my family I can trust without reservation.

3. Limits to my behavior.

4. People who encourage me to be independent.

5. Good role models.

6. Access to health, education, and the social and security services I need.

7. A stable family and community.

### I Am

1. A person most people like.

2. Generally calm and good-natured.

3. An achiever who plans for the future.

4. A person who respects myself and others.

5. Empathic and caring of others.

6. Responsible for my own behavior and accepting of the consequences.

7. A confident, optimistic, hopeful person.

### I Can

1. Generate new ideas or new ways to do things.

2. Stay with a task until it is finished.

3. See the humor in life and use it to reduce tensions.

4. Express thoughts and feelings in communication with others.

5. Solve problems in various settings—academic, job-related, personal, and social.

6. Manage my behavior—feelings, impulses, acting-out.

7. Reach out for help when I need it.

# The Road to the Resilience Model

It took many years for resilience to be recognized in human behavior. The biggest obstacle was the notion that people were the result of a good or bad environment. If you were lucky and had a good environment, that is, no problems, lots of support, great education, money, and so on, you would be a good person. If, by contrast, you had a bad environment, that is, poverty, a dysfunctional family, poor education, and so on, you would be a bad person. This is an adaptation of what is called the "pathological model." It comes from the medical model, which assumes that the best way to deal with problems is to diagnose and treat them. It was believed that social problems could only be solved through diagnosis and treatment.

Researchers using the pathological model uncovered, much to their dismay and confusion, what was finally recognized as resilience. Researchers such as Emmy Werner in Kauai, Norman Garmezy in Minnesota, and Michael Rutter in England were conducting studies of the impact of poverty, mental illness of a parent, or the effects of alcoholic and dysfunctional parents on children. They assumed that the children would be negatively affected by such an environment and would present behavioral and health problems similar to or directly related to those of their parents.

What the researchers found instead was that about one-third of the children in each study were not "damaged" by their parents' illnesses or self-destructive behavior. These children were well adjusted, happy, had friends, and, in follow-up studies, continued to be happy and well adjusted. As a matter of fact, Emmy Werner, reporting after Kauai's Hurricane Adrian (1993), found that the children from her study, now adults, survived the disaster with less negative impact than others. Even their homes survived better—they had boarded up the windows in preparation for the predicted disaster. They had also invested in good insurance. (Werner's study began in the 1960s and followed up on the participants for more than three decades.)

What happened to the notion that children were shaped by their pathological environment? Garmezy and Rutter, so committed to the pathological model, first thought they must have misdiagnosed the parents and families. Werner was bewildered by her findings, and wanted to explore for some better answers.

To the credit of these fine researchers, they shifted their focus: how were those children, the one-third making it, different from those children not making it? This is when the resilience factors began to show up—the same factors described in the resilience paradigm: I have, I am, I can. This paradigm organizes the resilience factors into external supports provided, inner strengths developed, and social and problem-solving skills acquired. Some of the terms used by the researchers include: trusting relationships, emotional support outside the family, self-esteem, a sense of being lovable, belief in God and morality, unconditional love, and ego-resilience.

The term "resilience" was not used consistently until the 1980s. The terms used prior to that, such as "vulnerable but invincible" or "protective factors," are, in fact, inaccurate. No one is invincible; everyone is vulnerable. The still-used term "protective factors" is especially inaccurate because resilience factors do not protect against adversities of life. People are not protected *against* but are prepared *for* the adversities of life—as demonstrated by the preparation of resilient adults in Kauai for the coming hurricane.

In contrast to the pathological model that focuses on individual weaknesses, the resilience model focuses on building an individual's strengths so that adversities can be faced and overcome. In the same vein, thieves or drug addicts sent to jail or a treatment center are best served if, while there, they learn to draw on resources, build inner strengths, and acquire social and problem-solving skills that help them deal with the adversities they are living with.

The whole person is the focus for overcoming adversities. We have come a long way in recognizing the grieving process after loss, the slow recovery process after abuse, the depression that accompanies chronic illness. We know that resilient people address these adversities more successfully than people who are not resilient, and usually recover more quickly.

# So How Do People Become Resilient?

A study I directed from 1993 to 1997, the International Resilience Research Project (IRRP), consisted of interviews with 1,225 parents and their children from twenty-seven sites in twenty-two countries around the world. Here are the main points I learned:

- Every resilient person was helped to become resilient. For young children, the major help came from those around them. As they developed over time, they increasingly drew on inner strengths and social and problem-solving skills. No one is born with skills or inner strengths.

- Temperament determines how an individual reacts to stimuli. Does the person react very quickly or very slowly to stimuli? This begins in infancy: how does the infant react to noise, movement, light, and handling? How is he best calmed down or energized? A person's basic temperament seems to influence whether the individual becomes a risk-taker or is more cautious and reflective. Each end of the temperament scale comes with strengths and weaknesses. The risk-taker does not always think of consequences before acting, loving to feel the adrenaline rush when testing limits or challenging the line between danger and safety. The cautious person does not always take action when it is necessary or even crucial.

- The promotion of resilience is influenced by the temperament of each person. Does he need to learn to manage impulsive behavior when confronted with an adversity? Does she need to learn to get psyched up when confronted with an adversity? Different strategies and dynamics in the use of resilience factors are needed for different temperaments. For example, families promote resilience in different ways. Some encourage autonomy and independence more than (and sooner than) others; some involve extended family members; some use empathy, help, and praise; and others use discussion, availability of family members, and displays of affection.

- Socioeconomic environment does not determine resilience. I found as much resilience in families from low-income environments as in high-income environments. However, people in high-income environments who had more education tended to use more resilience factors in promoting their resilience. (For example, they could afford to use professional services not financially available to other families.) However, this difference did not necessarily make them or their children more resilient. As a matter of fact, many families at the lower end of the socioeconomic scale were incredibly resourceful in dealing with adversities. They pooled resources, took over child care so parents could find work in another town, or hid food so that there was something to eat during extreme financial trouble.

- Many studies indicate that average or above-average intelligence is necessary in order to be resilient. The study I directed found no such thing. No single resilience factor indicates resilience. For example, the studies citing academic achievement as the indicator of resilience may be looking at single-factor indicators of resilience. It is not uncommon for some researchers to assume that a single factor such as self-esteem or social skills indicates resilience. There are programs today that continue to focus on single factors as indicators of resilience. I found that, as will be elaborated later, it is the dynamic interaction of a number of resilience factors (from the "I have, I am, I can" paradigm) that indicates resilience. Many, many children who are not very successful in school or, indeed, have no formal education, are resilient. And many parents who had no education are resilient and know how to promote it in their children. Resilience is more complex than one factor.

- Cultural variations are a factor in determining the different dynamics for promoting resilience. One culture praises children as they find their own solutions to problems; another provides loving support and helps children face an adversity; resilience is promoted with both styles. Between cultures there are also differences in actions that prevent the promotion of resilience, for example, severely punishing children, making children overly dependent on outside help, or expecting children to solve their own problems without bothering others. Children experiencing such actions often become depressed or ill, run away from home, or distrust or fear adults. Only if they are able to promote their own resilience or find help elsewhere do they become resilient in spite of the negative actions.

- The age of a child is related to resilience. The younger the child (roughly speaking, under eight), the more the child depends on outside resources (the "I have" factors) to become resilient. The older the child (eight and up) the more the child promotes her own resilience through acquired skills (the "I can" factors). The inner strengths (the "I am" factors) continue to develop and strengthen over the lifetime.

- I found that there is a gender difference in children's development of resilience. Girls draw more on seeking help, sharing feelings, and being sensitive to others as they face an adversity, while boys are more pragmatic, focusing on the problem and the possible outcomes of various actions. Girls begin to use resilience factors to help others face adversity at a younger age than boys—as young as five or six. They show more empathy, offer more help, and share more feelings than boys when dealing with an adversity.

## The Focus Is on You

This book is about you and promoting your resilience. It will help you:

1. Build on your present strengths.

2. Strengthen your present weaknesses.

3. Reexamine previous experiences of adversity.

4. Prepare for coming experiences of adversity.

5. Apply resilience in a variety of settings.

6. Make decisions about using your resilience to help others.

Building your resilience quotient is important because of the role the factors outlined in the test play in your ability to face, overcome, and be strengthened by—or even transformed by—experiences of adversity. When you have support, inner strengths, and skills to deal with problems, you are in a better position to face the adversities of life. If you lack supports, if you have inner doubts about your value as a human being, or if you have not acquired interpersonal and problem-solving skills, then you lack the vital tools that can help you.

You started on your road to becoming more resilient when you determined your current resilience quotient. You now have a picture of which resilience factors are strong, which are weak, and, perhaps, which you do not have at all at the moment.

This book will help you look at your life and examine or reexamine earlier experiences of adversity. Doing so will help you recognize who contributed to (or prevented) the promotion of your resilience as well as determine what *you* contributed to (or did to prevent) your resilience.

The first part of this book examines the experiences you most likely had as you were growing up. Your overall development coincided with the development of resilience factors. They were not separate. Their role now is to help you face, overcome, be strengthened by, and even be transformed by experiences of adversity. You still draw on what you learned at each developmental stage. In learning more about your early development, you can reexamine your experiences and see if you need to do anything to change the effects they had on your life. Is something missing that needs to be added?

The second part of this book describes the role of your resilience in different settings, different relationships, and different times of your life. It also includes strategies for promoting your resilience as you determine the need.

The third part covers how to prepare for, live through, and learn from experiences of adversity.

Enjoy the journey!

# PART ONE

---

Examining and
Strengthening
Your Resilience
Building Blocks

# I

---

# Trust

Whatever resilience you have today did not just happen. It is the result of experiences you've had in your life beginning as early as your birth, perhaps even before birth. These experiences usually began in the family, and could only be understood by you as you grew and developed. You could not understand, for example, a feeling such as empathy—feeling someone else's pain—when you were a baby, but you could understand a feeling of trust. Trust, in fact, is the first stage of your development and is also the first building block of resilience. It is the very foundation of resilience! So, let's start with trust.

Trust is a trait that indicates you can trust others with your life, your needs, and your feelings. It also indicates you can trust yourself, your abilities, your actions, and your future. Trust cannot be measured by the behavior of others—rather, it deals with the feelings you have toward the people you trust, primarily the feeling of love but also the feelings of security, comfort, and well-being. There are also feelings connected with trusting yourself. You feel good, happy, and proud when you trust yourself to take a chance on trying something new or trust yourself to show love to someone without being overcome with fear of rejection.

# Building Trust: In the Beginning

Trust began to develop during the first year of your life, and its development was promoted by one or two people, usually your parents or another caregiver. But trust in yourself was developing at the same time. You were learning to trust your ability to work out a rhythm of feeding with your parents and to trust that they would provide what you needed. You learned to trust that your parents would take care of you when you were hungry, wet, needed love and comfort, or were afraid or angry. You were learning to trust your ability to calm yourself and increasingly manage your body. You were learning how to turn yourself over, sit up, crawl, pull yourself up, and walk, but with assistance. You also learned how to grasp, hold, and pull.

Think about how dependent you were on your parents or other caregiver when you were a baby. You certainly had to trust them. Your very survival depended on trusting others, but not just any-one—only those to whom you felt emotionally attached. You needed to be emotionally attached, or bonded, to the ones you trusted. Trust-ing and loving go hand in hand. At any age, good feelings—not nec-essarily love, but certainly caring or appreciation—accompany feelings of trust. If you could not trust your parents or another care-giver to meet your basic needs, then you could only feel vulnerable to whatever harm came your way. You were helpless in the face of your adversity: neglect. This would form the basis of having no trust in your parents. But, because you were so helpless and could do little yourself to meet your needs, you would also lose trust in yourself. With such loss of trust in your parents and in yourself, it would take very little to finish the picture of mistrust to include everyone else, the world.

The price of not learning to trust is great. Your present feelings of trust in others and in yourself are built on your early experiences. While you cannot recall those early experiences that shaped your feel-ings of trust and the accompanying love, you can begin to think about where you are today in terms of your feelings of trust in others and in yourself. As you reflect on your current status, you may find it helpful to consider some of the reasons parents do not provide the trusting relationship infants so desperately need.

Why would parents not help to develop trust in their baby? Why would parents not meet their baby's needs? Are they cruel peo-ple? Are they ignorant? Are they self-centered? Here are some of the most common reasons parents give for not providing the care and love their baby needs:

- their own fatigue;

- feeling overwhelmed with the constant need to care for the baby;

- finding it hard to care for more than one child;

- going through abrupt changes in their life; and/or

- experiencing a return of issues from their own childhood, such as too many bad memories.

Other reasons given by parents are related to the behaviors of their baby:

- screaming, crying, or whining;

- not sleeping through the night;

- not performing as well as the parents think their baby should;

- touching everything; and/or

- clinging to the parent who has to leave for work.

It would be difficult to underestimate the stress that many parents, very likely yours as well, experience. This is especially true for new parents, who often have difficulty making the transition from relative freedom to the total dependence of an infant. Even with the inevitable falling in love with the baby, there is stress in the new demands.

Many parents quickly realize that their negative feelings and behaviors can harm their baby. Perhaps she cries more, doesn't smile, doesn't reach for anything or respond to anything, or even avoids looking at the parents as a result of the negativity it senses. With the help of family and friends, through reading about child development, or just by testing ways to reduce the undesired behaviors in their infants, such parents would learn to:

- show patience,

- make a game of tasks,

- soothe and reassure the baby,

- offer attractive alternatives and choices,

- maintain realistic expectations,

- provide solutions,

- encourage continued efforts, and/or

- praise efforts and success.

These actions would promote both the trust the baby has for the parent and also the trust within herself that the baby is developing.

Here are two examples: one involves an infant needing a trusting response from a parent, and the other involves an infant needing to build self-trust with the help of a parent. The first infant expresses the need for a trusting response by screaming, crying, and whining. The challenge is to determine what the behavior is telling the parent. The baby could be saying any of the following:

- I am physically uncomfortable.

- I need someone to soothe me.

- I need some loving, especially by touching, rocking, singing, or holding.

- I am upset because I feel unloved.

- I feel I cannot trust you to be there when I need you.

A response that would reassure the infant and help the parent through the situation while promoting trust would be, "Oh, my, you are unhappy. Let's see what's wrong. I don't see anything. Maybe if I hold you and sing to you . . . I love you so much. I wish I could comfort you. I wish I knew what was wrong. I'll stay here until you calm down." The time spent performing this kind of response helps the parent calm down, helps the infant calm down, and reestablishes trust in the infant. Easier said than done, right?

Suppose the other infant is not performing as well as the parent wants, because the parents expectations exceed the baby's developmental abilities. The infant may be upset and frustrated because he cannot meet the parents demanding standards. Perhaps he regularly winds up with a dirty face when eating, which the parent finds undesirable. Surely, she thinks, the baby can be trained to be a neat eater. A response that would reassure the infant and help the parent through the situation while continuing to promote trust would be, "Let's see. I guess it's really hard to eat without getting your face all dirty. I'm probably expecting too much from you. You're really trying hard. Let's get a wet towel to use, and I'll mash the vegetables, okay? I'll bet you'll get more in your mouth that way!"

These kinds of responsive answers make life easier for the parents, the infant, and for the promotion of trust, which is the overall focus of this age group. Try to recall the earliest experience you had with your parents that promoted your trust. It is important for you to go back as far as you can because early experiences over which you had little control inevitably influenced the role of trust in your life. Exploring them now will help you understand how. Trust me!

Think of an experience you had with a parent in which you were aware that your parent was contributing to the promotion of your sense of trust—in your parent, in yourself, and in the world. What was the experience? Describe it in as much detail as possible in the blank lines that follow. Here are some guiding questions to get you started.

- What happened?

- What did you do?

- How did you feel?

- What did your parent do?

- How do you think your parent felt?

- How did the situation come out?

With your full description of the event in mind, now focus more on the implications of that event for the resilience building block at hand: trust.

- What did your parent do or say that helped you build trust in your parent, in yourself, or in the world?

- What did you do as part of that experience that promoted your trust?

- What did you do at that time that may have prevented the promotion of your trust?

_____

_____

_____

_____

_____

_____

_____

_____

With your better understanding of the role of trust in your life and how it helps you become more resilient in the face of adversities, what can you do now that will promote more trust in yourself and in others? What decisions can you make? What actions can you take? You may want to think of some other experiences with trust that occurred with your family, and ask yourself the same questions.

# The Continuity of Trust

Trusting yourself and others is a basic need that continues throughout life. It plays an increasingly important role in your ability to face and deal with the many adversities you will encounter, because you cannot deal with adversities if you don't trust your own ability to do so or you don't trust anyone else to help you. Nothing is more damaging to your core self than to have no trust or to have your trust betrayed. Your reactions to such lack of trust are dangerous and damaging, as the following examples demonstrate.

- Without trust you may try to control others. You may reason that people who cannot be trusted are dangerous and potentially hostile, but if you can control them, they cannot harm you.

- Without trust you may withdraw from human interaction. Perhaps withdrawing makes you feel safer and less threatened by the world.

- Without trust you may become overly self-reliant and independent, to the extent that you close down your emotions and keep your distance if someone is nice to you.

Now let's look at some of the things you may do as a result of not trusting *yourself.*

- You may not fully develop your abilities. The reason for this is quite clear: if you cannot trust yourself to achieve, then you will protect yourself from what you perceive as inevitable failure. You'll let others do things for you and will become dependent, often on people who are overly controlling. Perhaps you are easily manipulated because you are certain that other people are better than you or know more than you do.

## *"I Have" Resilience Factors Related to Trust*

As the basic building block of resilience, trust continues to be the foundation of resilience and continues to play an important but changing role in your life over time. Of the resilience factors listed in the introduction, which ones require trust for their successful development?

### Limits to My Behavior

When you trust someone, you are more willing to accept their setting of limits to your behavior. You trust them to have your own interest in mind, and trust them not to want to prevent you from doing things that are safe and appropriate. You feel you can trust them to talk to you, to negotiate limits, and to explain why the limits are set. Or you can even trust them enough so that they do not need to give specific reasons. Here is a situation where that kind of trust became crucial:

A nine-year-old boy, Ben, wanted to play with a friend who was unacceptable to his family, and was furious when he realized his mother did not trust his judgment to select his own friends.

*Mother:*   I don't want you playing with Joey. I've told you that before, and it upsets me when you continue to play with him. He isn't the kind of person I want you to play with.

*Ben:*   Well, I like him. He's fun and I like to go to his house. He has his own room and we can play alone.

*Mother:*   That's just it, honey. I don't want you in his home. There are some problems there, and I don't want you getting involved.

*Ben:*   What kind of problems?

*Mother:*   You'll have to trust me on this, honey.

*Ben:*   But I like Joey and I want to play with him.

*Mother:*   Well, I guess it would be okay to let him come over here. You invite him over here and tell him your mother needs to have you at home, that there is a rule about your being home after school.

If Ben did not trust his mother, he might have continued to play with Joey, whose father was a heavy drinker and had been arrested for attacking his wife and Joey. Ben's mother was afraid her son might get caught in such an attack if the father came home drunk. She was reluctant to share that information with her son, because she did not think he could handle it. In this exchange his mother, in addition to asking him to trust her, helped Ben understand the rules by restating them, showed her feelings and concern for his welfare, and negotiated a solution to the problem. Each of these behaviors added to his sense of trust in her caring about him and his welfare.

## Good Role Models

When you trust someone, you are willing to see that person as a good role model. You trust the person enough to imitate how he or she behaves. This is especially important when you imitate the behavior of a role model as you face an adversity. An interesting example of this is the story of a ten-year-old boy who learned that even good role models might behave unpredictably if they are under stress. The boy was at school and his teacher had been a role model for what to do in the event of an earthquake. She had told each class member to follow certain behaviors if an earthquake came, and she would lead them when the earthquake hit. But when the earthquake did hit, the teacher fled in panic. The boy, remembering what she said and not what she did, became the role model for the other students in how they should behave.

This is an important story because it incorporates two major points concerning the promotion of resilience. One is that memories of what role models do or teach are helpful even when the actual role model falls apart. Second, the story shows that kids as young as ten are learning to promote their own resilience. Children under the age of eight or nine rely primarily on others to promote their resilience; children after that age increasingly promote their own resilience. They rely on trust in others to help them, but they can draw on trust in themselves, and are learning that the memory of what others have modeled for them can be applied toward their dealings with adversity.

# "I Am" Resilience Factors Related to Trust

## A Person Most People Like

Trust and caring go hand in hand; there is really no separating the two. So, in order for you to feel trust in others, you must feel that others care about you, like you, and will not harm you.

## Empathic and Caring of Others

If others care about you and demonstrate their care, you can trust that your caring about them will be accepted. And the trust in others helps you become sensitive to their feelings, which is what empathy is all about.

## A Confident, Optimistic, Hopeful Person

When you develop trust in others, you become more self-confident and have increasing trust in the future.

When twelve-year-old Jack and his younger cousin got lost exploring the woods near their home, those three "I am" factors came into play. Jack had taken his cousin deeper into the woods than ever before and it began to get dark. It was time to head back for home, but where was the path? Jack couldn't find it. He was scared and could see his cousin was too. So the first thing Jack did was tell his cousin he was sorry that he was making him afraid and understood his fear. ("I am empathic and caring of others.") Next, he assured his cousin that he would find the way out for them. ("I am a confident, optimistic, hopeful person.") It was getting darker and darker but Jack did not lose courage, even though he wanted to cry. Finally, he saw some familiar buildings and told his cousin they were safe. In this case, trust and caring played major roles in overcoming the adversity of being lost and preventing the younger child from panicking.

## "I Can" Resilience Factors Related to Trust

### Express Thoughts and Feelings in Communication with Others

When you trust yourself and others, you are more willing to share feelings and thoughts and more able to benefit from such interactions. You are not afraid that people will betray your confidences or take advantage of what you reveal to them.

### Solve Problems in Various Settings

Your sense of trust in others and yourself allows you to address the inevitable adversities you face in life. You trust you have the resources available and the skills and self-confidence needed to deal with the adversity.

### Reach Out for Help when I Need It

Your trust in others gives you the confidence to reach out to them when you are dealing with an adversity. You feel secure that they will help you, can be trusted to give you good advice, and care about you.

On eight-year-old Pat's first day in a new school, his mother was quite ill and was unable to take him to school; he would have to go alone. This was particularly scary for Pat because he had always attended a small country school until now—this was his first day in a big city school. When he got to the school and didn't know what to do, he became a new target for teasing by the other kids. He felt humiliated and cried, which brought more taunts. But when he saw a teacher come out of a building, he immediately drew on his ability to reach out for help. He told the teacher he was new and didn't know where to go or what to do. He also explained that he was crying because he didn't like the kids laughing at him. He trusted her to help him, and of course she did. She took him to his classroom and introduced him to the teacher, and the teacher picked up from there. It was only a matter of days before he made friends.

# Resilience Factors and Trust

Resilience factors alone will not enable you to face, overcome, and be strengthened or transformed by experiences of adversity. Rather, the dynamic interaction of resilience factors applied to an experience of adversity is what works. For example, you may have had a trusting relationship with your parents, but perhaps you were not allowed to explore your environment for fear of harm. This prevented you from feeling a sense of self and the joy of learning new things on your own. If you *were* allowed to explore, the dynamic interaction of trust, confidence, and problem-solving probably helped you deal with the adversities of falling down the stairs or bumping your head on the stool.

In promoting resilience, there is no *one* pattern of the dynamic interaction of resilience factors. There are many and they may be changed at any time. But some patterns are used more frequently than others and are used more frequently by some people than by others. One common pattern found in my study is this: the child has a loving, trusting relationship with the parent (I have); the child feels lovable (I am); and the parent and the child communicate in their own way (I can). The dynamic interaction of these resilience factors is what works. Note that resilience factors from each category need to be used to deal with adversities; one factor from one category won't work. Other patterns will be described in the next chapters.

# Trust in Teens

The continuity of trust is especially volatile and at risk in the teen years because that is the time of dramatic changes in development. Those changes occurred as part of your development and affected the choices you made about whom to trust as well as your sense of trusting yourself. Some of these changes are listed below.

## Trusting Peers More Than Family

The desire to be accepted by peers and the increasing desire to be independent of parental control easily lead teens to a kind of blind trust in what their peers do.

## Trusting Yourself in an Inconsistent Way

The insecurities of the teen years are many. You did not always know if you could be trusted to carry out a task, get a good grade, or be accepted on the team. You were especially vulnerable to distrusting yourself in your new interest in members of the opposite sex. Could you trust the object of your interest to respond in kind or would that person reject you or humiliate you? Did you trust yourself to try again with someone else? Your swings in trusting and not trusting yourself were probably distressing and required a new kind of attention. Such ambivalence about trusting yourself could be tested when what you trusted yourself to be able to do was in conflict with what your parents felt about it. For example, Janice, age sixteen, is very excited about having a date with a college sophomore. She tells her parents about the date, an invitation to a college dance. Her parents are stunned by this announcement. "No way," her mother says. "We don't want you dating someone in college, much less going to a party there."

"But, Mom," yells Janice, "I'm sixteen years old. The high school guys are so immature."

"That will be enough!" shouts her father. "You're not going and that's the end of it."

Janice cries and runs out of the room.

The parents were obviously surprised at the sudden announcement from their daughter. They had no preparation for it and reacted before they had a chance to think about it. It is very difficult for most parents to see their children become more independent in their decision making, especially when they see that risks are involved.

What could Janice's parents and Janice herself have done to see the situation as an opportunity to maintain the trusting relationship between them and also build Janice's trust in herself? Here's an alternative dialogue.

*Parents:* This certainly is a shocker. We never thought you would be making decisions like this without giving us some earlier indication of what might be coming.

*Janice:* Well, I feel I can make decisions on my own and that you will trust my ability to make good ones.

*Parents:* We certainly don't intend to make you feel we lack trust in your ability to make good decisions. But you need to understand our concerns. We are concerned about what some of these college students do at parties. We do not know if there are any older people there who would make sure nothing happened to harm or embarrass the guests. We don't know if you have thought enough about getting out of a bad situation if things go wrong. We just don't know how prepared you are for taking care of yourself.

*Janice:*    I can see your point. I really would be confused if things went wrong, like my date getting into a fight or someone getting drunk and bothering me. Maybe we need to talk about some rules for dating.

*Parent:*    Good. That's what we need to do. But we need to do it right away, if you are to keep this date! We don't want to prevent you from going to the party, but we would feel much better if we all agreed on some rules. How about these:

One. Always carry enough money with you to call home and ask to be picked up, or to call a taxi.

Two. Always agree on a time you will return home and make sure the date accepts that time.

Three. Always explain to us who will be at the party.

Four. Always provide the address and phone number of where the party is being held.

## Limits of Trust

Trusting others does not mean trusting everyone. There are many people who cannot be trusted or they might try to exploit you, cheat you, lie to you, or betray you. So, one of the limits of trust is to recognize whom not to trust. When you were very young, you relied on others to tell you whom to stay away from, but as you developed more trust in yourself you also developed greater ability to assess other people. Perhaps you are now in the habit of comparing new people to people you already trust, or perhaps you know how to observe their behavior and question how trustworthy they are.

Think of an experience you had in which you were involved with someone who turned out not to be trustworthy. What was the experience? Describe it in as much detail as possible in the blank lines that follow. Here are some guiding questions to get you started.

- What happened?
- What did you do?
- How did you feel?
- What did the other person do in response?

- How do you think the other person felt?

- How did the situation come out?

With that full description of the event in mind, you will now want to focus more on the implications of that event for your sense of trust in yourself and the resulting limits you feel in trusting others.

- What did the person do that made you decide he or she was untrustworthy?

- What did you do (what actions did you take and what decisions did you make) to prevent any damaging effects on you from what happened?

- What did you do (what actions did you take and what decisions did you make) that may have aided and abetted the person in taking advantage of your trust?

- What can you do now that will help you increase your ability to gauge those you can trust and those you cannot trust?

_____

_____

_____

_____

_____

_____

_____

_____

_____

# Filling the Gaps in Your Trust

If you feel you don't have trusting relationships or don't trust yourself to deal with experiences of adversity, then you need to take action now.

Look around you. Think about someone you know or know about who could help you build trust in yourself and others. Do you have a friend, a relative, a teacher, a counselor, a mentor, a neighbor, or someone at church who can help? When you do your search, you may want to ask yourself the following questions:

1. Will this person respect my confidence?

2. Will this person listen and be empathic?

3. Will this person give me suggestions?

4. Will this person continue to help me?

Any time you trust, you are vulnerable. Someone may betray your trust, take advantage of it, make fun of you, tell others, or use what you tell them against you. These are real risks. But in order to become resilient, you must take risks. You cannot deal with many adversities alone. You need to trust others and you need to take the risk of trusting yourself.

I heard the following story from a man in a workshop I conducted. "When I was in the fourth grade, my teacher beat me and abused me. I was terrified and in great pain, but I did not know how to stop it. I just allowed it to happen. I felt very sad and very angry, but helpless. Finally, when it was becoming too much, I told my parents, thinking they would help me get it stopped. But they refused to believe me and said I was a troublemaker. They were mad at me."

A child in the fourth grade, about age nine, is able to promote his own resilience, though of course he should not have to deal with such a terrible adversity alone. But this boy had parents who were unable to provide a loving, trusting relationship, so he had to trust himself to deal with the impact of the adversity he faced. He found help by observing role models of caring people. He did not want to get too close to anyone until he felt he could trust them, but his thinking and observing helped him realize that there are trustworthy people out there who are good role models for helping people who have experiences such as his. He was, in fact, transformed by the experience. The inability of his parents to provide a loving, trusting, and helpful relationship was a shock, but he made a decision that influenced his entire life. He decided he would become the kind of person who tries hard to help or save children in need. And that is exactly what he did: he became a school counselor for children at risk for dropping out of school.

Being resilient does not protect you from pain and suffering. Pain and suffering, however, can trigger resilience responses that help you face, overcome, and be transformed by experiences of adversity.

# 2

## Autonomy

The second building block of resilience, which develops around two or three years of age, is autonomy. Autonomy is the growing realization that you are separate from other people. You are separate from your parents, your brothers and sisters, everyone else. This realization allows you to understand that what you do can get responses from those around you and, in turn, they can get responses from you. You are a person. You are somebody. You see other persons, but aren't ready to see them as being as much of a somebody as you are. The self-absorbed, self-important ego is developing!

## Building Autonomy: In the Beginning

Your autonomy developed with a great deal of help and support from those around you. Your knowledge that you were a separate person and that you could influence and affect the behavior of those around you gave you a sense of power you did not have before. You could scream, "No!" and really get a response. You could refuse to let anyone dress you, and get a response. With your new sense of autonomy, you also became aware of your independence—the two go together. You were learning about autonomy through walking, throwing, pulling things apart, and opening doors and drawers. Sometimes you wanted to feed yourself, dress yourself, and decide whether or not to apply your toilet training. You could use some words to assert your will and declare your autonomy and independence. At other times you didn't want to do any of these things.

All two- and three-year-olds act this way. They need to, so they can become strong individuals who know who they are. But mistakes made during this time can cause problems in later years with how you feel and act.

Making mistakes can be a learning experience or a shameful experience. You had difficulty becoming autonomous and independent if you were not allowed to make mistakes or were criticized for trying to do things on your own. If that happened, you may have felt shame for your mistakes. That may have started a pattern of doubting your abilities and feeling incompetent. Of course, you may not recall those early experiences that shaped your feelings of autonomy and independence, but you can think about where you are today. As you think about your current status, you may find it helpful to consider some of the reasons parents and family members do not encourage autonomy and independence, so necessary to development and to promoting resilience.

Why would any family prevent a young child from becoming autonomous and independent? Are they afraid of the child? Are they afraid the child might get hurt? Don't they like the child? Some of the most common reasons parents give for not promoting autonomy in their young child include:

- fatigue from chasing after the child,

- fear that the child will be injured,

- feeling incompetent as parents,

- feeling embarrassed by the child's unruly behavior, and/or

- feeling a loss of freedom.

Other reasons are associated with the child's behavior:

- having temper tantrums, sometimes in public;

- knocking things over;

- throwing food and objects;

- crying, whining;

- running away from the parents or into the street;

- yelling or screaming at the parents; and/or

- refusing to talk or use the potty.

# How Does This Relate to You Now?

This phase of autonomy and independence inevitably set up a power struggle between you and your parents, which in turn began the life-long struggle you may be feeling concerning limits of behavior and freedom. This influences your future relationships with all kinds of authority, whether with the law or with people. Such early experiences really do have far-reaching implications for your life.

Many parents do not feel they should set any limits to their children's behavior, their free expression of their independence! Their concern is that they might crush the child's self-confidence in expressing and developing autonomy. Those around the child must, therefore, accept whatever the child does. But if a child is going to learn to be aware of the rights of others, he needs to accept limits to his own behavior. ("I have limits to my behavior.") Many preschool and kindergarten teachers find themselves in the role of introducing limits for the first time in the child's life, which is painful for everyone.

Many parents realize that their negative feelings and behaviors harm young children. Some children become passive and will not do anything unless a parent shows approval. Some children cry for hours in frustration and anger at being prevented from exploring the house. No one is happy in homes such as those. But with the help of friends and other family members, books, or just testing ways to reduce the undesired behaviors in the young child, parents can learn to:

- set limits,
- divert the child's attention,
- restate rules,
- offer help,
- state consequences,
- provide choices,
- help the child verbalize feelings,
- express their own feelings,
- stop the unacceptable or dangerous behavior,
- make a game of tasks,
- use humor,
- show patience,

- encourage the child to try, and

- praise efforts and cooperation.

Can you remember any of these actions being taken with you? Think back as far as you can and try to remember what your parents did to promote your autonomy and independence while setting limits to both. You'll come back to this after you have an opportunity to read some examples of what other parents did in situations that tested their patience and skills in promoting autonomy.

A mother and her two-year-old are in a store at a checkout counter. The little girl reaches for a bag of candy and starts to open it. The mother takes it away and tries to put it back on the shelf. The toddler grabs it again, screaming, "Mine! Mine!" The mother feels terribly embarrassed and angry. She has to decide whether to act out her own feelings or deal with her little girl. It is necessary to let the child know the limits to her autonomy. But she can also help her become interested in something else. The mother wants to calm her child and let her know she understands how much she wanted the candy, but that it is not good for her to have it or to grab things. The mother wants her child to know how she feels about the behavior. She wants to make clear that there are limits set and Mother sets them! So, she tells her daughter that although she cannot have the candy, she can have a Popsicle as soon as they get home.

Another child, a young boy, is knocking things over and throwing things because he seems frustrated in trying to build a tower of blocks. He may just be interested in exploring what if feels like, sounds like, or looks like to throw things. Or, he may be frustrated because his father doesn't know when to help him. Of course, the father has no idea what is causing the behavior but knows this is an undesirable situation and must be dealt with. The child must learn about limits to behavior. But, if autonomy and independence are to be built, the child needs to have freedom to explore, touch, and move things. How does the father handle this situation despite not knowing exactly what's causing the behavior?

First, the father states the rules: "No, we don't do that. We don't throw blocks. If you need help, ask me. You know how to use the blocks without throwing them." Then, he points out the emotional reaction if his son were hurt: "You wouldn't want to be hit by a block, would you? No, of course not." This promotes empathy for himself, with potential empathy for others. Then, he offers help: "I know it's frustrating to build a tower. Can I help you? We can put more on the bottom." Finally, he states the consequences of repeating the behavior: "If you throw blocks again, I'll have to take them away from you."

A general guideline to help build autonomy in children while also setting limits is to focus on the consequences of the autonomous behavior. If there is no great danger, the child is free to act. If there is some danger, the child is alerted. If there is a lot of danger, like playing with a knife, the child is stopped.

Now, look back as early as possible and remember experiences you had with a parent in which you were aware that the parent was contributing to the promotion of your autonomy and independence while also setting rules and limits. You may also want to recall an experience in which you were aware that your autonomy was not being promoted and that the rules were too strict, preventing you from feeling like an independent person. What was the experience? Describe it in as much detail as possible in the blank lines that follow. Ask yourself the following questions:

- What happened?

- What did you do?

- How did you feel?

- What did your parent do?

- How do you think your parent felt?

- How did the situation come out?

With your full description of the event in mind, now focus more on the implications of that event for the resilience building block at hand: autonomy.

- What did your parent do or say that helped you build your sense of autonomy?

- What did you do (what actions did you take and what decisions did you make) as part of that experience that promoted your autonomy?

_____

_____

_____

_____

_____

_____

With your better understanding of the role of autonomy in your life, the need for such autonomy, and the need for limits and rules, what can you do now that will promote more autonomy and a better use of limits and rules? Think in terms of the role of autonomy in resilience. You need a sense of autonomy, but you need to know what the limits are of what you can do in the face of adversities of life. As you accept rules and limits, you also accept the fact that you are responsible for what you do. Promoting autonomy and a sense of independence, as with trust, are basic to the promotion of resilience. Those who do not become autonomous, who have no sense that they are separate from others or that they are responsible for their own behavior, can blame others for whatever goes wrong. This will prevent them from developing a sense of responsibility for what they do. Where do you fall on the following continuum of blaming others for what you did?

1. It wasn't my fault, he did it.

2. It wasn't my fault, she started it.

3. It wasn't my fault, he made me do it.

4. It was my fault. I'm sorry.

5. It was my fault. I won't do it again.

6. It was my fault. I really learned a lesson from that!

As with trust, you are vulnerable when you act in an autonomous, independent manner. You must risk making mistakes, getting into trouble, having unexpected consequences, or failing. The comfort of blaming others is not even available. But becoming autonomous gives you a sense of freedom and empowerment you cannot get from others. You face others with a sense of being your own person who has the strength and courage to deal with the adversities of life. You are willing to risk the consequences and may, indeed, turn to others when you feel you cannot deal with life's adversities alone. You are independent but not isolated.

You can build your autonomy by recognizing that everyone makes mistakes and that we learn from them. Everyone fails at something and failure is a source of new knowledge. It's okay to make mistakes, to fail. They are not a judgment of you; they are experiences of life to learn from. A good way to look at your need for independence is to look at it in relation to your need for dependence. As you examine where you need or want to be independent and where you need or want to be dependent, you will discover a great concept: interdependence.

# The Continuity of Autonomy

Once you had autonomy and trust, you had two critical aspects of who you are, what you can do, and what limits there are to your freedom. You had two building blocks for becoming resilient. But you did not stay two or three years old. You kept developing and kept increasingly incorporating autonomy and trust in your development. In the previous chapter you saw which resilience factors were connected to trust. Which of the factors are connected to autonomy?

## *"I Have" Resilience Factors Related to Autonomy*

### Limits to My Behavior

Some aspects of limits of behavior have already been discussed, but it needs more attention here because it is an inevitable corollary of autonomy. Home and school were the two places where you had many experiences of the frequent conflicts between developing and expressing your autonomy and understanding and accepting rules and limits of behavior. Think about your home and your school and begin to recall experiences that involved the conflict between your autonomy and rules. If your parents and your teachers were controlling rather than encouraging of autonomy, then your ability to manage your own behavior and your overall ability to deal effectively with experiences of adversity were undermined. That is a terrible price to pay for too much external control. Here's a look at what parents and teachers can do instead:

- balance control and the need for autonomy;
- negotiate the limits of autonomy with children;
- insist on compliance, when necessary, but listen to objections;
- involve the children in setting limits and establishing rules; and
- appreciate the goal of children learning to manage their own behavior.

In this conflict between a father and his eleven-year-old son Russell, the son is using words to attack his father because he sees that words upset his father, and that makes him feel more autonomous. He may, however, be upset because his father never seems to listen to him and dictates orders or argues instead.

*Father:*   Hey, what's going on here? Why are you arguing with me? We have a problem—let's talk about it.

*Russell:*  I don't want to talk to you. You just don't listen to me.

*Father:*   Well, I'm sorry, but we don't seem to keep on any subject without an argument. Now, what started this argument?

*Russell:*  You didn't hear me when I said I had to do a book report this afternoon and couldn't take care of Cissy and Ray while you went to your office. You just insisted that I take care of them. That's when we started to argue.

*Father:*   Okay, I can see I didn't really hear you. Now, we still have a problem. I must go to my office for a while, and Cissy and Ray need some attention. Do you have any ideas about how we can solve this?

*Russell:*  Well, would it be okay if you took Ray with you? Cissy is easier to take care of and she can play with the new building logs while I write my report.

*Father:*   Sounds good to me. Let's do that.

Russell's complaint about not being listened to was respected in this resolution and the father pointed out a specific behavior of Russell's that needed to be changed (arguing). He reinforced Russell's need for autonomy by asking for his help in solving their problem. The resolution was sealed with praise for cooperation.

When Greg, fifteen, returned home from high school he greeted his mother with a smile. She didn't respond. He asked, "What's wrong with you?" His mother replied, "I just had a phone call from your counselor, and she told me what happened yesterday at school."

*Greg:*    What are you talking about? Everything's cool.

*Mother:*  No, everything is not cool and you know it. Stabbing someone in the shoulder in a fight is not cool.

*Greg:*    That's not true! You don't know what happened.

*Mother:*  The counselor told me plenty!

After this explosive interaction, Greg's mother realized she was not helping him deal with his apparent out-of-control behavior. So she decided to help him calm down as well as calming down herself. She suggested they sit down and talk about exactly what led up to the stabbing. As Greg talked, his mother urged him to express his feelings, especially when he realized his behavior was out of control. Then she talked about how she felt when the counselor called her and how afraid she was that he apparently lost control of his behavior. She helped Greg realize that he could have walked away from the boy instead of stabbing him. The conflict occurred because the boy kept poking at him, daring him to fight. "Things would be really cool," she said, "if you set limits for what you do when someone is provoking you." She also suggested they could spend some time learning some verbal defenses that would prevent things from getting out of control. Greg and his mother both met with the counselor to talk about the stabbing and to discuss what needed to be done and what Greg should do and say to the boy he stabbed. The mother helped Greg promote his understanding of limits of behavior and provided suggestions for alternative actions.

## "I Am" Resilience Factors Related to Autonomy

### A Person Who Respects Myself and Others

Because you know you are a separate person and that others are affected by what you do, you want to behave in a way that shows them respect and you want them to show respect for you. Showing respect for yourself and for others means you will not let anyone mistreat you, prevent you from becoming autonomous, or try to control you more than is necessary. Knowing how you regard yourself and want to be regarded, you see the desirability of showing respect and high regard for others.

### Empathic and Caring of Others

Empathy and caring about others are crucial to autonomy because you increasingly have the power to assert yourself, to take actions for or against others. The person who has no feelings for others or sees them only as obstacles is dangerous and, potentially, lethal. If trust was not developed enough to include feelings of empathy, such feelings are harder to develop after you become autonomous (but they *can* be developed). The best way to teach this to a child or youth is by helping him recognize his own feelings in a similar situation.

### Responsible for My Own Behavior and Accept the Consequences

This, in many ways, is the crux of autonomy. You must be responsible for what you do. You must be able, even if not willing, to accept the consequences of what you do. Autonomy develops around the same time as your conscience, your sense of right and wrong. No one really likes to admit he or she was wrong; that is why it is so easy to blame someone else. Who likes to pay for a speeding ticket, even when they know they were speeding? Lawyers are hired to prevent or minimize the consequences of actions that caused harm. Denial is also a common way to avoid taking the consequences of a harmful act. "I wasn't there," or, "I don't remember clearly. I don't know what you are talking about."

You cannot become resilient, however, if you cannot recognize your role in dealing with an adversity. If you are not able to assess whether what you do to overcome the adversity is useful and effective, you cannot overcome the adversity. You may deny it exists. You may say it is someone else's adversity to deal with, not yours. You have not been able to recognize your role and your responsibility as adversities are faced.

There is a continuing conflict between autonomy, seen quite rightly as freedom, and responsibility. Rules and limits are established so that the limits of freedom are clear. Responsibility for behavior is assumed to go along with freedom. Too many people still don't understand this concept.

## "I Can" Resilience Factors Related to Autonomy

### Manage My Behavior—Feelings, Impulses, Acting-Out

The autonomous person who assumes responsibility for what she does inevitably must learn to manage her feelings, impulses, and acting-out. If you want the joys of freedom, you must realize that such freedom is joyful to everyone else as well. You cannot violate their freedom for your own. Your behavior, expressed in actions, should not interfere with someone else's behavior.

# Resilience Factors and Autonomy

People develop different patterns for promoting resilience. You already read about one sort of pattern in the chapter on trust. Here is another pattern I discovered in my research: the child is encouraged to become autonomous (I have), the child becomes autonomous (I am), and the child is able to solve problems (I can). These particular resilience factors work together to deal with adversities and focus heavily on the role of autonomy.

Think of an experience you had that involved autonomy and some of the aforementioned related resilience factors. This may take some time to recall, but perhaps you already thought about an incident or two as you were reading this section. What was the experience? Describe it in as much detail as possible in the blank lines below. Ask yourself the following questions:

- What happened?

- What did you do?

- How did you feel?

- What did the other person do in response?

- How do you think the other person felt?

- How did the situation come out?

With that full description of the event in mind, now focus more on the implications of that event for your autonomy and the related resilience factors.

- What did your parent or someone else do or say that helped you build your sense of autonomy and the related resilience factors?

- What did you do (what actions did you take and what decisions did you make) as part of that experience that promoted your autonomy and the related resilience factors?

- With your better understanding of the role of autonomy in your life, what can you do now (what actions can you take and what decisions can you make) that will promote more autonomy and the related resilience factors?

# Integrating Trust and Autonomy

You have explored the roles of trust and autonomy as they began to be promoted within you at a very young age, and as they influenced your later development and your ability to deal with experiences of adversity. Now, let's look at how these two basic building blocks of resilience work together as you face and overcome experiences of adversity. Again, here are the resilience factors that affect the development of trust and the development of autonomy.

For trust, they include:

- limits to my behavior;

- good role models;

- a person most people like;

- empathic and caring of others;

- a confident, optimistic, hopeful person;

- express thoughts and feelings in communication with others;

- solve problems in various settings; and

- reach out for help when I need it.

For autonomy, they include:

- limits to my behavior;

- a person who respects myself and others;

- empathic and caring of others;

- responsible for my own behavior and accept the consequences; and

- manage my behavior—feelings, impulses, acting-out.

Notice the similarities and differences in the resilience factors involved with trust and autonomy. In particular, note that the factors "limits to my behavior" and "empathic and caring of others" connect to both trust and autonomy, while the other factors are either related to one or the other. That will change as the next building blocks are developed. Resilience increasingly incorporates and promotes *all* of the factors. It is the integration of the building blocks with the other resilience factors that allows greater flexibility in addressing experiences of adversity.

The following story was reported to a group during one of my workshops. See if you recognize the resilience factors associated with trust and autonomy that were used.

A law-enforcement woman walked into a game room used by troubled youth and saw a girl with a gun. The girl had been in a fight outside in the parking lot, and was eager to harm her enemy. The policewoman felt a rush of strength as she grabbed the weapon to keep it from firing. Then, when the situation was under control, the policewoman felt a weakness come over her that almost caused her to faint. Everyone else in the game room kept quiet and did not move or say a word. They expected the policewoman to handle the situation. Besides, they were frightened. They kept quiet until the girl was removed from the room. After it was over, the policewoman said, "I felt as much in control as I ever have."

While this book focuses on the promotion of *your* resilience, it is helpful for you to identify resilience in other people. Two things can result from seeing what others do. First, you learn the many ways people successfully or unsuccessfully deal with adversities. Second, you can explore how you would handle the same dangerous situation were it to occur to you. And, as a bonus to others, you might even think about how you could help someone who is facing an adversity. To that end, reexamine the resilience factors associated with trust and autonomy and identify those that contributed to the policewoman's ability to handle this serious adversity. Using the ones listed above, check off which were used in this situation. What did the policewoman and the others in the room do to demonstrate those factors?

Would you have done anything else in a similar situation? Have you had a similar experience?

# 3

## Initiative

The third building block of resilience, which develops around four or five years of age, is initiative. Again, the importance of your early experiences cannot be overestimated. Four and five are transition years that prepared you for separation from your parents and entry into the real world: school. During these transition years, you developed an increasing ability to promote your own resilience. People around you continued to play a part in promoting your resilience, of course, but at that age you were just beginning to have a say about what happened in your life. The role of initiative at this time refers to the growing interest you had in starting new things, becoming involved in many activities, and reaching out to be part of the activities of others. You experienced a growing realization that the world is one great field of activities and you could be part of it. You wanted to try everything!

## Building Initiative: In the Beginning

You developed your initiative, as most children do, by starting all kinds of activities and projects that you didn't necessarily complete. Too many other things attracted your attention. You most likely wanted to help family members and friends with their activities. And, many times, they saw you as invading their turf. The important thing was that initiative was generated by you. You no longer looked to your parents or others to stimulate your interest. You saw what was exciting, what appealed to you. Your autonomy and independence joined to give you a sense of being ready to start things on your own.

You began to figure out what symbols stand for and you asked endless questions about anything that tapped your interest. You spent considerable time involved in all kinds of play, especially pretend play. And you probably had some difficulty separating fantasy from reality, lies from truth. But fantasy is the beginning of creativity. It is the main source of new ideas, inventions, and individual talent.

If you were not able to take the initiative to accomplish things, especially because you were rejected by those you wanted to help, you would tend to feel guilty for doing something wrong. Or you might have felt unworthy of love and attention. Or, you might feel you were a naughty, even bad, person because you were scolded so much for being into everything and not accomplishing much.

You can probably remember experiences from the age of four or five; many people have vivid memories of experiences during those years. But, even if you can't, you can think about where you are today. As you think about your current status, you may find it helpful to consider some of the reasons parents and family members do not encourage initiative, so necessary to development and to resilience.

Why would any family prevent a child from taking the initiative in activities? Don't they want to be bothered by the child? Is order in the house more important than the development of the child? Some of the most common reasons parents give for not promoting initiative in their child include:

- tired of nagging the child to clean up;

- anxious about keeping their job, no time to consider the child;

- dissatisfied with their child-care arrangements;

- fear for their child's safety in the neighborhood;

- problems with their spouse or close friend;

- doubts about raising their child properly;

- angry about criticism of child-rearing by relatives; and

- a sense of facing endless problems with no solutions.

Other reasons are associated with their child's behavior:

- shouting angry words, calling names, swearing;

- hitting, throwing objects, grabbing, biting, spitting;

- teasing siblings;

- refusing to share, take turns, or play by the rules;

- arguing, lying to cover up actions;

- refusing to listen, tuning adults out; and

- dawdling while eating, dressing, and/or going to bed.

Parents don't usually set out to inhibit their child's initiative; they are simply too overwhelmed and preoccupied with their own problems. The child becomes one more burden. Fortunately, many parents realize that their negative feelings and behaviors harm their child. Some children withdraw from doing anything because they feel guilty for making the parents so unhappy. Some children feel they're bad because they seem to need so much scolding. Some children feel they are unworthy of trying to be helpful—no one wants help; it's rejected every time. But through talking with friends, reading books, visiting preschool facilities, or working out by trial and error more effective ways to promote initiative in their child, parents can learn to instead engage in some of these behaviors:

- offer help;

- respect their child's feelings;

- describe behavior that needs changing;

- restate rules;

- stop unacceptable or dangerous behavior;

- teach alternatives, using such words as, "what else can you do?";

- praise efforts and successes;

- invite the child to express his or her feelings;

- get the child's attention;

- insist on cooperation;

- accept apologies;

- give a time frame for completing a task;

- express their own feelings about the child's unacceptable behavior; and/or

- involve the child in solving the current problem.

# How Does This Relate to You Now?

You may not know what problems your parents had when you were four or five years old, but you can probably recall some of the behaviors that your parents scolded you for. What kinds of activities did you engage in that you remember were praised by your parents? What kinds of things did you get involved with that brought criticism, or even punishment from them? Look again at the list of things parents can do to promote initiative in their children, and check off the ones that you recall your parents or someone else using with you.

Your memory may be jogged by reading some examples of what other parents have done to deal with the unacceptable or annoying behaviors of their four- and five-year-old children while still promoting their initiative. Initiative is a critical resilience factor; it motivates people to find new ways to solve problems and initiates action to deal with adversities.

A five-year-old girl, Sylvia, is quite willing to argue, tell lies, or break rules, because she wants to be free to work on her latest project. She does not like being expected to do chores and be a responsible member of the family and she feels very guilty for being caught not doing what she is expected to do, so she pretends she has done her work.

*Mother:*   I certainly am upset when you tell me you finished cleaning up your room and I can see toys and clothes everywhere. You didn't even put your dirty clothes in the hamper.

*Sylvia:*   It's clean. I just forgot a few things.

*Mother:*   No, that is not acceptable. You know how to clean your room—you've done it before. So do it now.

*Sylvia:*   I can't now. I'm making a bird's nest out of string and I need to find something to put it in. Why do you want me to clean my room when I'm busy making something?

*Mother:*   Oh, so you have a new project. That looks very hard and very fun! I'd like you to show me how to do it, but first you need to finish cleaning your room. Remember, chores come first.

The mother wants Sylvia to know there are expectations of her behavior, so she clarifies them again—probably for the fiftieth time, but she will continue to do so as long as the expectations continue to need restatement. The mother also points out the undesirable tactics Sylvia uses to avoid doing what is expected of her, and lets her know that they are not acceptable. But her mother also respected Sylvia by recognizing her interest in a project. This kind of response shows love and respect for Sylvia but makes clear that certain chores must be done and are not negotiable. The relationship between mother and daughter is not impaired because Sylvia's initiative in developing projects is not ignored. In addition, Sylvia is recognized as a person who is able to accept responsibility for taking on certain tasks in the family. She is an important, necessary member of the family! Sylvia has structure and rules in the home (I have), is expected to be responsible for what she does (I am), and is expected to manage her own behavior (I can).

Another situation describes a four-year-old boy, Chris, who does not want to listen to his parents and tunes them out instead. They seemed to make unreasonable demands on him. He is busy and does not want intrusions on his activities.

*Father:* You must be in outer space. You're not hearing a thing I'm saying. Look at me, Chris. What is going on so you're not listening to me?

*Chris:* I just want to play.

*Father:* Well, I can understand that, but we need your help in setting the table. So please don't tune me out. When you do that, I feel upset and hurt that you would completely ignore me. That is not a nice way to treat me.

*Chris:* I'm sorry, but I wanted to finish my puzzle.

*Father:* Okay, you have ten minutes to finish the puzzle. Then, set the table.

The father used a number of responses to avoid attacking Chris' need and desire to engage in activities that were promoting his initiative. He got Chris' attention by focusing on him with clear language. He insisted on cooperation from Chris. He accepted Chris' apologies, because after all the child was really honest about wanting to play instead of work! Finally, he compromised with Chris by giving a time frame for ending the play before accepting his responsibility to the family, which shows empathy with what Chris really wanted to do.

Now, look back on an experience you had when you were four or five years old that involved your taking the initiative in starting an activity or trying to get involved with someone else's activity. What was the experience? Describe it in as much detail as possible in the blank lines that follow. Ask yourself the following questions:

• What happened?

- What did you do?

- How did you feel?

- What did your parent do?

- How do you think your parent felt?

- How did the situation come out?

With your full description of the event in mind, now focus more on the implications of that event for the resilience building block at hand: initiative.

- What did the other person do or say that contributed to your ability to take the initiative?

- What did you do (what actions did you take and what decisions did you make) as part of that experience that promoted your initiative?

- What did you do (what actions did you take and what decisions did you make) at that time that may have prevented the promotion of initiative?

_____

_____

_____

_____

_____

_____

_____

With your better understanding of the role of (and the need for) initiative in your life, what sorts of things could you do differently? Think especially in terms of the role of initiative in resilience, because you need to be able to take the initiative in dealing with the adversities of life. Being passive, feeling you are not worthy of consideration, or feeling guilty for bothering others—all these feelings inhibit you from taking the initiative. Consider those negatives and see how they played out in the situation you described above.

The promotion of initiative, as with trust and autonomy, is an essential building block of your resilience. At four or five years of age, you could begin to find others who could help you with the blocks that need building. Many of the children in my study found to be resilient in spite of living in dysfunctional families had gone to someone outside the family to find trust, a sense of autonomy, and freedom to take the initiative in all kinds of activities. The outsider was usually a grandparent or other relative, but sometimes it was a teacher from a preschool program, a neighbor, or even a friend. Can you remember someone outside your family who played such a role with you? What did that person do to build your trust? What did that person do to build your sense of autonomy? What did that person do to help you develop your initiative? People are not limited to the influences of their family. There are others who often can provide what parents are not able to. You can become resilient in spite of your family experiences.

# The Continuity of Initiative

The earliest stages of your developing initiative affected your future in terms of your creativity, your leadership, and your ability to generate ideas and actions. Part of promoting resilience is connecting your initiative-related skills with the other resilience factors.

## "I Have" Resilience Factors Related to Initiative

### One or More Persons I Can Trust and Who Love Me without Reservation

You need someone who gives you a supportive environment where you can try new things, ask questions, and feel safe as you engage in your projects. We joke about the artist or writer who lives off of friends and never seems to work. But it is just such support that leads to some of our great cultural treasures. Most people don't need total support, of course, but helping someone find the time for a project and encouraging them is very important and helps build their initiative.

### Limits to My Behavior

The limits of behavior as they relate to initiative are a continuation and expansion of the limits of behavior for the development of autonomy that you learned about in the previous chapter. These limits were more difficult for you to accept when you were four or five, but now you can reexamine what you remember about being four and five, and think about how you developed during those years. Can you remember who set the limits? How did they set them? Can you remember your feelings about such limit setting? Think about how limit setting affects what you do even today. Do you submit to limits? Do you challenge them?

### People Who Encourage Me to Be Independent

Your independence grows as you are successful in the results of taking the initiative. Those around you who encourage you to try again and not give up, and who praise your successes, are helping you increase your independence. As noted earlier, if you did not have such encouragement in becoming independent during the development of your sense of autonomy, you had more difficulty with the initiative stage.

## "I Am" Resilience Factors Related to Initiative

### Generally Calm and Good-Natured

Being calm and good-natured helps you tolerate the frustrations of having so many activities going on, annoying so many people, and wanting freedom to do all the things that invite your initiative. People who are easily upset or frustrated are confrontational when prevented from engaging in activities and will have difficulty promoting their initiative. Think about your temperament. Are you easily annoyed, do you have a short fuse, do you complain about being interrupted? Does that kind of reaction influence what happens to your taking the initiative? Perhaps you've lost interest in starting something new because you anticipated being frustrated and annoyed about it. Perhaps taking the initiative was too upsetting to bother with.

### Empathic and Caring of Others

At four and five years of age, you were becoming increasingly aware of other people's feelings. You would pet a dog, comfort a crying baby, and sense when someone was sad. You were aware of your own feelings and were better able to name them and thus name the emotions another person expressed. You understood enough about the connection between cause and effect to know your friend must be feeling pain when he fell down and scraped his knee. You recognized when your parents were unhappy and you may have put your arms around your mother when she cried or seemed sad. Perhaps you had an animal to care for who you loved very much. If he became hurt or ill, you wanted to help make him better. In terms of initiative, you were probably particularly sensitive to the feelings of empathy your parents expressed to you when you failed at a project. You needed empathy then and you recognized it when you received it—not by its name, but by the feeling.

Think about your empathy and caring for others. Are you sensitive to other people's sad feelings, or did you learn to ignore those feelings because you might intrude on their privacy? Taking action to help someone who is suffering has its risks, as does accepting empathy from others. Some people feel they might be perceived as weak if another person has to show empathy or offer help; some confuse empathy with pity and resent the emotion. Boys and men who have been taught that they are tough certainly don't need comfort from someone else, do they? Can you recognize when you would like to have someone comfort you? Perhaps you faced an adversity that was very painful to you emotionally and you needed comforting. Did you receive it?

### Responsible for My Own Behavior and Accept the Consequences

Again, this resilience factor was important for autonomy. But at ages four and five, there was much more to be responsible for, such as cleaning up the messes you made and completing chores around the house. You were also responsible for the consequences of your behavior. But you had greater powers during this period of developing initiative. You could explain your behavior. You could argue about or negotiate alternative solutions to the problem you created. You might have even suggested an appropriate punishment!

Think about your sense of responsibility when you were younger and, especially, now. Is it difficult for you to accept responsibility? Do you lie sometimes to avoid certain consequences? Do you have difficulty being criticized for taking the initiative? Do you become very defensive when justifing your behavior when you initiated an activity or made a decision that adversely affected others?

### A Confident, Optimistic, Hopeful Person

Self-confidence was not yet one of your strong points at the time that you first developed initiative. Much of your confidence came from the way other people treated you, the way other people reacted to the initiatives you engaged in. As explained earlier, if they criticized you, made fun of your projects, or scolded you for wasting your time on "useless" activities, you did not develop the self-confidence so important to resilience.

As your confidence was promoted, you could become optimistic about your future in initiating new projects and ideas. Even with failures, your confidence, optimism, and hopefulness would generate a sense of assurance that things would come out okay.

Think about these feelings now. Do you feel confident when you start something new? What shakes your self-confidence? Are you afraid of failure? Are you afraid of being made fun of? Are you afraid of being reprimanded? To what degree does failure threaten your optimism that you can succeed? Does disapproval make you lose hope that you will succeed? Think about these things and determine where you can add to or change these negative feelings. Can you practice alone until you are sure you know how to start and complete a task? Can you talk to someone you trust and tell them how little confidence you have in your ability to start something? That person may be able to help you. Focus on analyzing the tasks involved in what you want to start, and make sure you anticipate the problems that are very likely to occur.

## "I Can" Resilience Factors Related to Initiative

### Generate New Ideas or New Ways to Do Things

This is fundamental to your development of fantasy, creativity, originality, and talent. Taking the initiative is all about generating new ideas and ways of doing things. From this resilience factor emerge the creative people of the world. As you developed, you were very vulnerable to having this resilience factor crushed by criticism, indifference, accusations, or even punishment for not doing what you were expected to do as part of the family. ("Stop playing! Get to work!") Unfortunately, people have a tendancy to divide work and play: work can't be play, and play can't be work. Nothing is further from the truth, but such a division is established at this very early age. The implication is that you cannot and should not feel joy and excitement in your work; you cannot and should not feel pain and frustration in your play.

What is happening in your life today? What do you do with your creative ideas? Do you share them, test them out, or do you decide they are silly or can't be done? Do you have people around you who encourage you to come up with new ideas? Have you ever participated in a brainstorming session devoted to generating new ideas? It is a great experience and worth pursuing both at work and at home. Many new ideas of how to deal with the inevitable adversities in life and in the world come from such sessions.

## Express Thoughts and Feelings in Communication with Others

There is a new power, beginning at four and five years old, in your ability to express your feelings. Of course, your feelings have always been part of your development, starting with the feeling of trusting love your parents provided and you shared. But later you found out that there exist *words* that described how you felt. You were more alert in recognizing feelings that others expressed. You picked up body language that communicated feelings, and you were increasingly aware of what could hurt your feelings and the feelings of other people. You were beginning the socialization process that would become increasingly important in addressing experiences of adversity. You also were learning how to express your thoughts about events and about what others were doing.

Where are you today in expressing your thoughts and feelings? Are you able to express an opinion on a topic or about an event? Are you comfortable enough to share your feelings with someone you know, or are you afraid of being betrayed or thought foolish? You really are not able to resolve conflicts if you do not know how to express thoughts and feelings. Have you ever practiced what you are going to say when you need to express your thoughts or feelings? Do you plan what words you will use and how they will sound to someone else? Rehearse with a friend and ask for comments. Sometimes, just a change of words makes all the difference: instead of, "Sorry, I can't help," you might try, "I wish I could help you, but I have to go to the school to pick up my daughter and I'm late already." Or, instead of, "You made a mistake that must be corrected," you could try, "There seems to be a problem here. Can you look at it again to see what it is and how it might be corrected?" Do you see the different responses you might get with the different ways of communicating? Practicing what you can say and how you can say it at home or in some quiet place enriches your relationships. The way you communicate with others will determine, to a great extent, their receptiveness to new ideas you initiate.

## Solve Problems in Various Settings

Do you take the initiative in solving a problem you experienced (or created) in the many projects you engage in? Such problem-solving skills enhance your ability to start new activities. Did you feel you could solve problems when you were younger? Or did you make repeated mistakes even when you knew the solution? Are you willing to risk making mistakes now? Are you willing to expose yourself to others by taking the lead in solving a problem a group faces?

## Manage My Behavior—Feelings, Impulses, Acting-Out

When you were four or five years old, you probably had trouble managing your behavior. You were probably disorganized and impatient, wanting to take action long before you thought through what you wanted to do. Where are you now in managing your feelings, impulses, and tendency to act out? Are you easily roused to fight with words or fists? Is your patience at the lowest possible tolerance level? Have you learned how to prevent yourself from becoming destructive when your impulse is to attack? Your ability to be patient in your interactions with others and with your own projects will influence the quality and acceptance of the things you initiate.

## Reach Out for Help When I Need It

When you were young you were probably so eager to do things on your own that you resented help. You wanted the fun of doing something yourself. As you faced problems that seemed insurmountable, you would reach out for help and accept it, but only if the helper didn't take too long or didn't try to finish the project for you!

Where are you today in reaching out for help? It is probably much easier, but you may still have feelings that you don't want to lose control of the project. Perhaps you are cautious about someone else offering more help than you really want. Many people who do not enjoy working with others fear intrusion into their territory. They want the pleasure and even the pain of their own initiatives. Do you find that while you want some help you want it pretty much on your own terms? Do you define what help you want and make sure that's all that is provided? Your ability to understand your feelings about reaching out for help is important to your ability to deal with adversities.

Here is a true story from a friend of mine that describes what happened to her as she was developing initiative.

> I had a tendency to lie when I was a little girl. I remember being punished for lying on several occasions. I lied about breaking an object, not doing what I was told. I was five years old when I apparently had lied once too often. Now, my father was a good man and I loved him, but he was the disciplinarian in the family and my spankings occurred when he got home at night. Waiting for them was painful and enduring them was more than seemed possible to handle. He would reconcile later, but the feelings of hurt remained.
>
> This time I clearly was seen as having hit his tolerance limit. He said I was so bad he would not let me live there

anymore. I was to pack up and be ready when he got the car and rang the front doorbell. I was to be taken some place else. My mother heard all this and did nothing. She stayed with me and said nothing. When my father rang that bell, I screamed in terror. He came into the house and said, "Will you behave after this?" Of course, I agreed. That was the end of it. But not for me. I learned that I had to accept the limits to my behavior or would be severely punished, even sent away. I learned that if I did what I was told, I could stay at home. So, my behavior determined if I was accepted or rejected. I learned that I could not count on support from my mother.

And then I discovered school. I learned that if I obeyed the teacher and if I tried very hard to please her, I would be accepted. I was bright enough to meet expectations, I worked hard to please the teacher, and I was very successful. I got great grades and teachers loved me. But as I grew up, I realized I did not have to obey or try to please others. If I pleased myself, I usually pleased others. I learned that it was my achievement, the quality of my initiated projects, that was important, though I hoped it pleased others too. It usually did. I frequently thought about my early experiences of punishment and realized my father thought he was doing the right thing. I still have some pain over it, but I can handle that.

When you think about that report, what do you see was lacking, not only in terms of developing initiative, but also her development of trust and autonomy? She gradually overcame this adversity and certainly showed resilience. But being a resilient person does not mean you don't suffer. You live with those painful experiences, overcome them, and may even be transformed by them. But the pain lives on.

# 4

## Industry

The fourth building block of resilience, which develops around the ages of six through eleven, is industry. Now you were taking on a larger society: school. You were responsible to and even dependent on teachers and the limits of the school setting. You were engaged in mastering two areas of your development: school subject matter and socialization within the school culture and with your peers. You wanted to be successful and have a positive self-image as an achiever; you wanted approval from your teachers and probably tried hard to please them with your achievement. You wanted peer acceptance and approval, and close friends. This required mastery of social skills.

## Building Industry: In the Beginning

Your early focus on school and peers meant your parents were now less important to your sense of achievement, acceptance, and approval. You became more interested in the school environment, where you were mastering academic skills. You were also learning a great deal about socializing with peers, sometimes in an organized, structured setting, and sometimes in a kind of free association. Your socialization outside the school also changed. You probably joined teams or scouts or church groups, and had different socializing experiences. You probably depended on your parents to drive you to these groups and events, but you did not need them as much for your development of the fourth building block of resilience as you did for the previous three.

## Inferiority Complex

How does industry affect resilience? Well, you have to be able to master skills so you can begin the process of solving problems associated with adversities. You first began to develop this ability at age eight or nine, when you were not so dependent on your parents or teachers as you had been previously. You learned to master some social skills so that you would be able to talk with others, share thoughts and feelings, use the support systems available, and reach out for help to deal with adversities. If you felt inferior to others, however, you probably tended to focus on your sensitivity to your limitations rather than on the adversities you inevitably faced in school. You may have felt inferior in mastering the skills school offered, or you may have felt inferior in socializing with your peers. This condition, the inferiority complex, begins to develop during these years.

If you were not successful in developing industry, especially mastery of school skills and socialization with peers, you very likely felt inferior and became extremely sensitive to your limitations. Your parents, teachers, and friends may have made fun of you or communicated in a variety of ways that you were not much of an achiever. These feelings of inferiority can remain throughout life and are barriers to resilience. You probably remember experiences from those years and may even think about them from time to time. You may remember successes and failures in your school work and in your relations with teachers and peers.

If you still feel inferior to others, you need to think about ways of removing that feeling. One way is by finding areas of activity where you can master the required skills. Computers have contributed an incredible sense of mastery with many adults. Or you may have a talent that can be developed and that you increasingly master, such as singing, dancing, painting, or making things. Many talents are not developed in the schools. Talents not consistent with the school curricula may or may not be developed in the home or supported by the family. This is where the resilience factor of initiative, developed earlier, comes in to play. Remember, new ideas, creative productions, and new solutions to problems all began during the years you were developing initiative. Think back and see where such creativity was stopped. Then, start to think of that "stopped" point as an adversity. You can draw on trust, autonomy, and initiative, as well as the related "I have," "I am," and "I can" resilience factors, to deal with these feelings of inferiority.

## Industry at Home versus at School

What are some of the reasons that school and even the home do not promote the development of industry? Parents are often dealing with their own problems and do not have time to be concerned about the problems their children are dealing with. Besides, the school may be seen as the place where children's development happens, not home. Perhaps the parents often let the children take the consequences of their behavior, solve the conflicts themselves, and learn from their mistakes, believing this is the best way for children to learn. This may work for some children, but it assumes children have the ability to define and solve their problems without adult help, which isn't usually the case. Most children do not yet have these skills and need guidance as they are developing and mastering them.

Teachers have problems, too. These frequently consist of fear of loss of control of the students, overcrowded classrooms, insufficient materials, lack of training in the subjects being taught, and lack of understanding of the social and emotional development of children. The problems the teachers have with students involve misbehavior in class, failure to do homework, fights, disrespect for the teacher, and inattention. These problems in turn lead to bad grades or detention, which are obstacles to the promotion of industry.

Both home and school have expectations of certain behaviors and values in children. These expectations differ from each other, and children are required to understand and accept and adjust to the many differences. Take a look at the things required at home and at school.

At home:

- a sense of responsibility
- feeling empathy and care for people
- expressing their thoughts and feelings
- resolving conflicts with family members and friends
- building friendships
- sharing, taking turns
- holding interests and skills independent of school
- having a sense of humor
- feeling confident

- being flexible
- increasing autonomy and self-management
- becoming socialized with nonpeers both in and outside the family

At school:

- a sense of responsibility
- self-control
- achievement and mastery of skills and subject matter
- group behavior and team work
- being accepted by peers
- showing respect for oneself and others
- sharing and taking turns
- listening to the teacher
- obeying rules
- accepting authority

Both home and school require a sense of responsibility and sharing. But some of the other expectations are different, such as feeling empathy and caring for people—the home promotes this and the school does not. A child who expects or displays empathy and caring in the school may be rebuffed or even teased for being such a "sissy." Children learn that what the home expects and what the school expects are different and need to be learned separately.

Another example of the differences concern relationships with people of different ages. At home, the relationships are across ages and the interactions respect and make allowances for these differences. At school, however, the relationships are with same-age peers and little interest in other grades is observed. Often, children who are older than their classmates are shunned.

Children must learn to negotiate both worlds. Parents and teachers are not actively involved in preventing the promotion of industry, of course, but their behavior is often in conflict with the characteristics they wish to promote and as a result, the importance of industry for learning to deal with the adversities of life may not develop.

In the research on resilience I conducted, only one-third of the parents or teachers were, in fact, promoting resilience in children. They did not use the word "resilience"; it is only recently becoming a word people understand and use. But the parents or teachers were not promoting the development of the qualities and characteristics they wanted in the children. There are a number of reasons for the contradiction. First, perhaps they knew what was desired but did not know how to help the children acquire the characteristics. Second, perhaps they did not prepare the children to apply resilience factors to situations of adversity beyond very familiar situations. For example, a child may learn to reach out for help only to a member of the family, and not be able to use that resilience factor with anyone else. Or, a child may learn how to deal with his parents working long hours but may have trouble dealing with his parents going away on a trip without him. A third reason for the contradiction is that parents and teachers often have difficulty remembering to promote resilience in children any time their own sense of loss of control of the children—or feeling threatened by them—takes over.

Select an experience you had that involved industry when you were in school sometime between the ages of six and eleven. Think in terms of what in that experience promoted or prevented the development of your industry. What was the experience? Describe it in as much detail as possible in the blank lines that follow. Ask yourself the following questions:

- What happened?

- What did you do?

- How did you feel?

- What did the teacher do?

- How do you think he or she felt?

- What was the outcome?

With your full description of the event in mind, now focus more on the implications of that event for the resilience building block at hand: industry.

- What did your teacher do or say that contributed to your ability to engage in industry, that is, master skills and become socialized with your peers?

- What did you do (what actions did you take and what decisions did you make) as part of that experience that promoted your industry?

- What did you do (what actions did you take and what decisions did you make) at that time that may have prevented the promotion of industry?

- With your better understanding of the role of industry in your life, what would you do differently in the same situation?

_____

_____

_____

_____

_____

_____

_____

Here is an experience a friend of mine related to me in which an eleven-year-old boy named Bob felt he was failing to master a certain skill that was important to him.

Bob was in a language-arts class instead of a foreign-language class, which he would have preferred. His parents spoke Spanish but had not taught it to him, and he had been to Spain but did not stay long enough to learn the language. He really wanted to learn the language.

He came home one day and told his mother that he was a dummy. He had heard a teacher say that the reason some students could not study a foreign language was because they couldn't read and needed to go the language-arts class instead.

*Mother:*  Well, Bob, what do you want to be when you grow up?

*Bob:*  I want to be a marine biologist. Or maybe a pilot or an astronaut.

*Mother:*  You are smart enough to do any of those things. Now, of the things you might want to be, do you think Spanish will help you?

*Bob:*  Well, no.

*Mother:*  It is important to read in any one of the interests you have. And math is important for some of them. You know you are great at math. You get top grades in it, and your teachers have told me how good you are. If you want to learn Spanish, we'll send you to Spain for the summer when you are sixteen or seventeen. You can stay with Uncle José. He would love that. You'll know more Spanish after three months than most high school graduates know after four years of Spanish.

*Bob:*      Really, why is that?

*Mother:*   Because you'll have no choice but to speak the language. It's called "language immersion," and it's really the best way to learn. So, get on with your reading!

In this situation, Bob's mother put her son's feelings of failure into the perspective of his great talent for math and her faith that he was smart enough to achieve any of his goals. She also pointed out how he could acquire the language skill he desired and how it could be done in a way that could be better than the school's method. And, finally, she reinforced the need for Bob to master the reading skills so important for everything he was interested in becoming. She was combating feelings of failure while promoting industry.

# The Continuity of Industry

The building block of industry, as with the other building blocks, helps shape your future in terms of how well you master and use skills related to your career or work as well as your interpersonal relationships. Industry by itself is a powerful building block, but it is enhanced through a connection with other resilience factors.

## "I Have" Resilience Factors Related to Industry

### Good Role Models

You learn so much from watching how other people tackle a difficult problem. Your teachers were role models, of course—you may even have learned which teachers were *not* such good role models because they were too authoritarian or not very interested in the students. Who were your role models? Who are your role models today?

### People Who Encourage Me to Be Independent

In chapter 2, you learned about the way you developed independence during your autonomous phase. Now, your independence is not just a declaration that you are a separate person, but a sense of being able to rely on yourself. If this was reinforced by your peers and teachers, your industry now is that much more powerful. Can you remember those who helped you become more independent?

## "I Am" Resilience Factors Related to Industry

### An Achiever Who Plans for the Future

Your mastering of academic and social skills was not just to please others, it was increasingly for your future. As you began to think about the future and realize that there is a life after school, you could plan for it. To what extent do you still plan for the future?

### Responsible for My Own Behavior and Accept the Consequences

You were building integrity as you were mastering academic and social skills. You increasingly saw the importance of accountability in both the process of mastering skills and in the products. Can you remember an experience in which you didn't want to accept responsibility for something you did related to the mastery of skills? Did you resolve it so you could feel a sense of integrity? If not, think about it now and decide what you should have done.

## "I Can" Resilience Factors Related to Industry

### Stay with a Task until It Is Finished

You can be interested in mastering new skills, but if you don't have the ability—the persistence—to stay with a task you'll of course have trouble mastering the skills.

### Solve Problems in Various Settings

You develop flexibility when you can transfer problem-solving skills from the academic and social arenas to the various adversities you face. The basic steps of problem-solving can be applied to any setting: identify the problem, discuss alternative solutions, modify solutions or come up with new ones, take action, judge outcomes, and decide what to do next.

### Reach Out for Help When I Need It

Your ability to reach out is dependent upon your ability to communicate your needs. (Communication is a topic discussed in detail in chapter 7.) Are you able to turn to others when the situation calls for it? Can you think of a project that didn't turn out the way you would have liked because you needed help but didn't ask for it?

# The School and Socialization

Developing social skills is a critical part of developing your industry, and school was the arena in which you developed a huge number of those skills. Unlike trust, autonomy, and initiative, social skills are acquired. The way you behave, the way you talk, and the way you approach people are all acquired skills. They are a major component of "I can." You acquire some of these social skills at home and some at school. But what I've found too frequently is that these things are not being taught in either place. In both places, children are often expected to learn these skills on their own by a kind of trial-and-error process. The home may be so informal that an outsider would feel uncomfortable. The school may feel that the students should be left to socialize on their own terms as they see fit. The result too often is children who suffer from a lack of social skills and therefore have difficulty using them to help deal with adversities. Such children grow into adults with exactly the same problem.

The home socializes at an intimate level. There is freedom to say and do things that cannot be said or done outside the family. There is the opportunity to test social behavior with siblings and parents without the risk of social isolation. There is opportunity to experiment with different behaviors such as how and when to compete and when to cooperate. There is little risk of being thrown out, expelled, or rejected by the family. A member may be teased or ridiculed, but is usually kept as a member of the family.

The school socializes in two ways: as part of the school culture and in the socialization of peers. The school culture develops over many years—students who change schools are very aware of this phenomenon because they sense a new culture in their new school. Rules are different; peer relationships are different. But there are some general overriding values and behaviors important to the school in the socialization of children. The critical ones are independence, cooperation, social competence, and communication.

## Independence (Autonomy)

This one is familiar to you by now—in chapter 2 you took a look at its development in your early years of life. Now you need it so that you can do your work, complete tasks, ask questions when something is not clear, assume responsibility for your work, and feel proud of your achievements. If you had trouble with this resilience building block as a youngster, you may find that trouble continued in school. Can you remember depending on others to help you with your work instead of being independent? Can you remember feeling insecure when you were expected to be independent and confident?

In chapter 2, did you determine any ways in which you can act to change your thinking and increase your sense of independence?

## Cooperation

You did not want to use this social skill back when you were developing your initiative for the first time. You were pretty much a loner then, except when you tried to "cooperate" with what someone else was doing! So, the skill of cooperation is a little late in developing, and much of it is learned in the early grades of school. Cooperation for students means working with other students to develop projects and carry them out. It implies that you know how to resolve conflicts in decision making and how to assess actions that are taken. Is someone moving too fast? Is someone trying to take charge? Is someone just riding along?

Cooperation also refers to students cooperating with the teacher. Teachers give assignments, set standards, and define expectations. Students are expected to accept the standards and complete the tasks. Children who had trouble with the limits set for their behavior in their earlier development have trouble cooperating with teachers. This has led to many problems for students, although some schools have worked to find a solution for both teachers and students. One of the satisfying developments in schools today is a program called service learning, which is for students who have trouble with too much structure and with external controls. In service learning, they are able to take the initiative in designing a project, alone or with other students. They provide some service to the community by determining a need, conducting interviews, analyzing responses, writing a report about the project, and then presenting it to some audience. Afterward they must reflect on what they did, how successful it was, and what changes should be made in the next project. This is an excellent example of the fact that there isn't just one way to promote industry. Flexibility needs to be introduced in the ways that people learn.

Did you have trouble cooperating with teachers and with other students? Perhaps you preferred and still prefer working alone, selecting your own topics and doing your own research, writing, and reporting. If you were required to work in a group, how did you feel about that?

## Social Competence

What is seen as social competence in the culture of one school may be very different in the culture of another school. Social competence involves such things as how to approach the teacher and other students, and how (or whether or not it's even acceptable) to approach other authority figures such as the librarian or principal. You are expected to know the power structure of the school and the limitations of your entering it.

## Communication

Good communication requires that students have the words needed to communicate. They are expected to be aware of how others respond to what they say and how they say it. It also assumes that the students understand the dynamics of conversations, the role of emotions, and the role of body language. To my knowledge (with the exception of class discussion on the communication styles of characters in a book), such communication skills are not taught in the schools. They are learned, for the most part, from interactions with teachers and with peers.

How did you learn your communication skills? Are you even aware of how you learned them? Look at the characteristics of effective communication listed below, and place a check mark next to those you possess. Place a different mark (such as an X) on those you feel you are lacking. The promotion of industry and especially the promotion of the resilience factor "I can reach out for help when I need it," depend heavily on your ability to communicate well.

- *Friendly and nonaggressive.* The tone and volume of your voice, your facial expressions, and the words you select all communicate friendliness and nonaggressive attitudes when you speak.

- *Expressions of affection.* Using words to show that you and the one you are communicating with like each other contributes to effective communication. For example, nicknames such as "girlfriend" or "bro" add to friendly communication. Expressions of appreciation for accomplishments, such as "Way to go!" or "Cool!" also communicate caring.

- *Assertion.* State clearly what you believe and what behavior you will accept from others. Clarify the limits of the interaction by knowing when, for example, to say no.

- *Seeking help and support.* Know how to ask for help when you have problems or need answers to questions. What words will describe what you need and why?

- *Respecting the space of others.* Recognize that everyone has a sense of personal space. This applies to groups as well.

Words such as "May I interrupt?" or "Excuse me, but this is urgent" work well.

- *Accurate perception of others' behavior.* Perceiving others' intentions and motives, and understanding the feedback they provide, is probably the most difficult skill to acquire. Many adults have trouble with this communication skill.

- *Listening.* There is much that interferes with listening. Do you find you have trouble giving your full attention to a speaker? All kinds of thoughts, from recent events to earlier experiences, have a way of intruding. Skill is required to focus on the speaker, process what is being said, and recognize the major points being made.

- *Sharing thoughts and feelings.* It is difficult to share thoughts and feelings when you have enough trouble identifying and formulating them. How can you share something that seems nebulous at best? Take time to practice recognizing and labeling your feelings. One effective way of doing this is to give a name to every feeling you have at any given time. Also, practice clarifying your thoughts so that when you want to share them, they have words attached.

In a bit, I'm going to ask you to respond to questions about your experiences with mastering subject matter and becoming socialized. First, however, you may find the examples described below helpful. These are examples of teachers who knew how to integrate their teaching of subject matter with socialization and communication skills.

Two sixth-grade boys, Sid and Jack, were fighting in the cafeteria. Sid's homeroom teacher heard about it from another student, so he confronted Sid the next day.

*Teacher:*  Hi, Sid. I heard about the fight in the cafeteria yesterday.

*Sid:*  Oh, that.

*Teacher:*  Now, I'm really upset by that information and am having trouble trying to understand why you fight with your friend Jack. Are you angry about something he's doing?

*Sid:*  Oh, Jack is a jerk. He goes around the cafeteria and takes food off our trays. When he got to me today, I was ready for him. I let him have it. He won't do that again.

*Teacher:*  That certainly was a bad scene, Jack behaving the way he did. Do you think there's another way you can stop Jack's behavior so you don't fight? You know, fighting is what little kids do because they don't know what else to do. Besides, fighting doesn't improve your feelings about Jack and what he does. It might not even stop him.

Sid:      He deserved what he got, and I think I'd do it again.

Teacher:  Where will that lead—fight after fight after fight? I'll bet you can think of something else to do. You know, maybe Jack is having troubles at home or with friends. Maybe he doesn't know any other way to show his frustration and anger.

Sid:      Well, he did say something about his parents divorcing. I wonder if that's what's bugging him. I really should talk to him.

Teacher:  That's a good idea.

The teacher's responses that promote communication and socialization include:

- expressing feelings and concern,

- encouraging the exploration of alternative solutions to the problem,

- pointing out consequences of unacceptable behavior,

- suggesting the use of empathy and altruism, and

- praising efforts to change behavior.

Here is another teacher who knew how to integrate her concern for subject matter with effective communication as she talked with one of her seventh-grade students. The student had not been doing her homework in arithmetic and her grades in math had been going down as a result. In concern, the teacher asked the student to stay after class.

Teacher:  Jean, I have been concerned about your not doing your homework lately and about your grades going down. Is something wrong?

Jean:     (Reluctant to say anything, looks down to the floor.)

Teacher:  Please, Jean, tell me what's wrong.

Jean:     Well, I think the class is very hard and I have trouble keeping up with it.

Teacher:  Oh, I'm sorry. But you haven't been doing your homework, either. I could tell from the homework you turned in last week what problems you are having. I can help you.

*Jean:*      Well, to tell the truth, I don't think you like me, and I wasn't sure you would help me.

*Teacher:*  (Laughing) You sure do have an open-and-shut case! Hard teacher gives low grades and doesn't like you! So you have no reason to do your homework and do your best in class. Now, Jean, who's getting hurt on this one? Me or you?

*Jean:*      (Also laughing) Not you, for sure. You know the answers. I guess I'm just hurting myself. But I really am having trouble with the math. Will you help me?

*Teacher:*  Of course I will. Do your homework tonight and tomorrow. I'll make sure to go over your work very carefully and point out where you are having trouble. Okay?

*Jean:*      Thanks a lot! I really appreciate this and I do want to get a good grade. (To herself: She likes me!)

The teacher's responses that promote communication and industry include:

- expressing feelings and concern,
- pointing out consequences,
- defusing excuses, and
- giving help when asked.

I once worked with a very troubled boy who did not want to go to school and, in fact, was not attending. When I met with the boy, it became very clear that he felt his father did not love him. This feeling blocked his ability to attend to his work at school so he just didn't go. No one at the school had seen the problem the boy was facing, though the school did call the father to find out where the boy was.

His father was, as a prominent lawyer, always busy helping those in trouble. When he came home, usually quite late, he was too tired to share time and communicate with his son. The boy, however, was communicating in his own way. As he left the room, I noticed in his back pocket a paperback book. I did not see the title of the book, but I did see that the cover had a picture of a father and son taking a walk along a river, with the father's arm around his son's shoulder. When I talked with the father later, I asked if he had noticed what his son was reading. He had not noticed, and was stunned when I explained how the boy was trying to communicate. He realized that he was not aware of his boy's need for a closer relationship with him. He realized he had no idea how his boy was trying to communicate. Clearly, he needed to help his son learn how to communicate with words. The complicating factor, however, was that the father felt he did not have time to spend with his son. It would mean giving up work that he felt he needed to do.

This is an example of the breakdown between what adults know they should be doing to help their children become resilient people versus what they actually do. How do they balance their own needs with those of their children?

Teachers face the same problem. They complain that they do not have time to be involved with problems or even the feelings of students. They point out their job is to teach subject matter, not to be involved with the feelings and problems of students. Yet these feelings are very much involved with learning. You learn best when you like what you are learning. Much of that excitement is generated in school by the teacher who recognizes the connection between learning and liking. Grades often reflect what excites students and what turns them off. School dropouts have declared their lack of pleasure in learning. They increasingly fail and do not like the feelings that go with being a failure, so they protect themselves from such unpleasant feelings by leaving. Do the teachers grasp the messages such students send them, or, like the father in the preceding story, do they become blind and deaf to the students' messages?

Now, try to remember another experience you've had, this time as an adult, that had an impact on your sense of industry. Can you think of an experience that used the dynamic interaction of a role model (an "I have" resilience factor), a confident and hopeful attitude (an "I am" resilience factor), and the seeking out of help (an "I can" resilience factor)? This particular dynamic interaction pattern of resilience factors was common in my research. It worked (and works) for many people.

What was the experience? Describe it in as much detail as possible in the blank lines that follow. Ask yourself the following questions:

- What happened?

- What did you do?

- How did you feel?

- What did the other person do?

- How do you think that person felt?

- How did the situation come out?

With your full description of the event in mind, now focus more on the implications of that event for the resilience building block at hand: industry.

- What did the other person do or say that contributed to your ability to engage in industry?

- What did you do (what actions did you take and what decisions did you make) as part of that experience that promoted your industry?

- What did you do (what actions did you take and what decisions did you make) as part of that experience that may have prevented the promotion of your industry?

- With your better understanding of the role of industry in your life, what would you do differently to promote its development?

_____

_____

_____

_____

_____

_____

_____

You are still learning to master skills related to industry. Your professional life requires skills—sometimes specific skills that require continual updating. Your interpersonal life requires the mastery of social skills, with increased flexibility as your social life expands. From your responses to the exercises in this chapter, you can see where you have been successful (or unsuccessful) in acquiring and applying skills related to industry. Hopefully, you can see where you need to give attention to changing what did not work and reinforcing what was effective.

# 5

## Identity

The fifth building block of resilience, which develops during the teen years, is identity. At that time, establishing your identity included two very important new aspects of your life: becoming sexually mature, and developing your higher mental capabilities of analysis and reflection.

## Building Identity: In the Beginning

The prevailing questions you most likely asked yourself during your teen years were these:

- Who am I?

- How do I stack up against other teens?

- What are my new relationships with my parents?

- What have I accomplished?

- Where do I go from here?

As a teenager, you were probably occupied with thoughts of who you are and how much you were appreciated by your family and, especially, by your friends. You wanted to be recognized as a unique individual with a clear and separate identity. You very likely wanted to appear competent and physically attractive. You wanted to be accepted and loved by those you loved, and you probably wanted to be considered popular and cool among your friends.

The benefits of establishing a clear identity are many. They include greater skills in:

- comparing your behavior with accepted standards;

- being helpful and supportive of others;

- reflecting on values, emotions, truths, and ideals; and

- integrating sexual interests with responsible behavior.

However, if you were not successful in establishing your identity, you may have experienced role confusion. You were not sure of your true personality and switched from self-assured to self-doubting. You may have felt alienated and were certain no one understood you, including yourself. Being humiliated or laughed at by others reinforced the role confusion. This was a real adversity for you: remember, adversities are real or perceived threats to your survival, your sense of security, your self-image, your sense of control, your social status, and your relationships with the family and, especially, with your peers. For teens, these issues directly affect the answers to the five questions posed in the beginning of the chapter.

# The Continuity of Identity

The building block of identity completes the five basic building blocks of resilience. It helps you define who you are and influences your self-image for most of your life. Identity alone is powerful, but it is enhanced and strengthened through connections with the other resilience factors.

As you read about each of the following factors, think of your experiences during those years and determine which ones promoted or did not promote your sense of identity. You may want to place a check mark next to the ones that apply and an X next to the ones that do not.

## *"I Have" Resilience Factors Related to Identity*

### One or More Persons I Can Trust and Who Love Me without Reservation

I still receive unconditional love from my parents or from someone else. I can always count on them to be there for me. They often tell me how much they love me and how proud they are to have me as their teenager. I trust my parents to love me even when I do something wrong or am in a bad mood. They try to comfort me and help me feel better. We can talk about what may be bothering me and they leave me alone when they know I am not ready to talk. I have trusting relationships with other people too, such as a teacher or other adult or a teen friend. I need these relationships to feel safe and secure.

### Limits to My Behavior

There are limits to my behavior that are negotiable as I show I can respect these limits. I am ready for more freedom. I like to be with my friends and I want increasing freedom to go where I want with my friends. I know the rules (and the reasons for the rules) for driving. My parents still set some limits on hours out and for friends that are acceptable versus not acceptable. There are still consequences when I break the rules, but we are able to talk in an adult way about what I did and why. Sometimes we negotiate consequences.

### Good Role Models

I still see my parents as models of how to behave in different situations. But I am more critical now and sometimes think they are not being fair. I can ask them why they did something and talk about it with them. I am becoming a more critical thinker and increasingly make decisions about who my role models should or shouldn't be. I increasingly shape my own ideas about how to behave.

### People Who Encourage Me to Be Independent

There is a continuing conflict with how much I need to be dependent on my parents to make my decisions. My goal is to become independent and responsible, but to draw on the help of others when I need it. I do not know everything and I am not invincible, so I need to be dependent at times. But there are people around me who encourage me to try to solve problems as much as I am able to on my own, so that I can grow to be more autonomous.

### Access to the Services I Need

I have schools, health centers, police and fire stations, and many social services that I can use. I feel secure when I know I can draw on outside services. I use them and my family uses them when we need help.

# "I Am" Resilience Factors Related to Identity

## A Person Most People Like

I am seen as pleasant and generally good-natured. I make friends easily or I focus on a few friends who like me. I try to do nice things to help people who are having problems. I am sensitive to how people are feeling and try to show my concern without seeming patronizing. I understand that people are more willing to accept me and help me when they see me as lovable, but I don't want to take advantage of that!

## A Person Who Respects Myself and Others

I respect myself and expect others to respect me. I am proud of who I am and what I achieve, and will not do things that make me ashamed of myself. If I do something wrong, I try to correct it so I feel good about myself again. I know others respect me because they can see I care about them as well as myself.

## Responsible for My Own Behavior and Accept the Consequences

My parents and teachers and friends have helped me become more independent by letting me make my own decisions and learn from the consequences. I know that I can do more things on my own but that my responsibilities increase, too. What I do affects what others do and the outcome of events. I can't blame others when it is my fault that things went wrong. I am also learning how to separate what I did to affect outcomes and what others did. This helps me know where the responsibility lies. I try to correct what I did wrong or apologize.

## A Confident, Optimistic, and Hopeful Person

I have confidence that things will turn out all right and that my future looks good. I accept my responsibility in making my future good. Even when I make mistakes, I have faith that things can be corrected and things will be all right. I know more about what is right and what is wrong because I can think more critically. But I am also aware that people do not always agree about what is right and what is wrong.

## *"I Can" Resilience Factors Related to Identity*

### Express Thoughts and Feelings in Communication with Others

I can talk with people about my growing independence, my future, what is expected of me, what my needs are, and what others want from me. I can discuss different points of view and negotiate solutions to problems in our relationships. I can communicate with my friends as well as with my family, and share my thoughts and feelings.

### Solve Problems in Various Settings

I am often able to see all sides of a problem and understand what it is about. This is true for problems that deal with my education as well as interpersonal problems. I can take the time to test out solutions with thoughts and words before I act. I am a more critical person than before, which means I am able to assess what someone else has done from a larger moral framework.

### Manage My Behavior

I am able to recognize my feelings and name them. I can usually recognize and label the feelings of others, too. Then, I try to find out what has made me feel like this or made the other person feel the way he or she does, because this helps me when I want to express my thoughts and feelings. By listening to the other person's thoughts and feelings I can show the person I care about his or her side of the conflict, and we can begin to resolve it. I try to manage any tendency to react too soon or too strongly, and to calm myself down and think before acting out impulsively. This is particularly true when I date.

### Reach Out for Help When I Need It

I can find someone I trust to help me. I am learning more and more to seek out those people when I am troubled, do not understand what is happening, or need to share my hopes and dreams. I can always go to my parents, but I also have others whom I can trust to help me.

Now, think of a particular experience you had when you were in your teen years that involved your sense of identity. Think in terms of what in that experience promoted or prevented the development of your identity. Ask yourself the following questions.

- What happened?
- What did you do?
- How did you feel?
- What did the other person do?
- How do you think that person felt?
- How did the situation come out?

With that full description of the event in mind, now focus more on the implications of the event for the promotion or prevention of the resilience building block at hand: identity.

- What did the other person do or say that promoted your identity?
- What did you do (what actions did you take and what decisions did you make) as part of that experience that promoted your identity?
- What did you do (what actions did you take and what decisions did you make) at that time that may have prevented the promotion of your identity?

_____

_____

_____

_____

_____

_____

_____

Which of the "I have," "I am," and "I can" resilience factors were used effectively in the experience you had? Which ones were not used well or at all? Which ones do you think still need strengthening? Remember, you don't need to use all of the resilience factors in dealing with an adversity. Different adversities require the application of different resilience factors. You may find some easier for you to use than others.

Here are some scenarios involving teens, with descriptions of what would promote (or prevent the promotion of) identity.

A fifteen-year-old boy left the house after his father told him not to. Identity would be promoted if the father talks to his son when he returns and asks him what the reason was for being late and breaking the rules ("I have"). The father should express his feelings of concern for his son's safety and how frightening it was for him when he could not find his son. The son can explain what happened and that he is sorry for what he did. The father needs to make clear that his son's behavior is not acceptable even with his excuses, and that he is responsible for what he did ("I am"). The father and son may negotiate a punishment and talk about what needs to be done to prevent this kind of behavior in the future. They can then reconcile ("I can").

Identity would *not* be promoted if the father yells at his son, telling him he is "no good and can't be trusted." The son then would feel guilty, but resentful of such a judgment. This would impact his sense of identity for a long time. The lack of discussion—expression of concern and fear for the safety of the son, explanations for breaking the rules, resolution, and reconciliation—makes sure resilience is not promoted. The son would learn that his father is cold, punishing, and not interested in working things out with him. His resentment would very likely remain and influence future behavior.

In another scenario, a shy, responsible, thirteen-year-old girl was torn between loyalty to her peers and her sense of right and wrong. "One of my classmates was cheating on an important examination. I told the teacher, even though I knew that the classmate and some others in the class wouldn't like what I did. I was angry with my classmate for cheating because it made things unfair for the rest of us. The teacher told the boy not to do it again and also called the boy's mother to tell her what happened. The boy admitted what he had done and promised not to do it again. I don't know if he knows I told on him, but I felt I had to report him." Identity would be promoted if she has a trusting relationship with the teacher ("I have"), if she feels some responsibility for the values of honesty and fairness and is willing to take the consequences of her behavior ("I am), and when she can analyze the conflicts she was dealing with and take action to resolve the problem ("I can").

Identity would not be promoted if the teacher tells the boy what the girl said or if the teacher had dismissed the girl as a tattletale. Resilience would not be promoted if the girl had ignored the cheating or did not reflect on the dilemma of the situation. Again, the establishment of identity in the teen years includes the new skills of developing the higher mental capabilities of analysis and reflection. The thirteen-year-old girl's dilemma is an example of this. Most importantly to the promotion of resilience, the girl needed to be willing to risk the negative reactions she feared.

A social worker who worked with gangs out in the street—in their territory and on their turf—recounted this experience. "The gang of sixteen-year-old boys had seven members that I know about. They had little to do and spent a lot of time dissing each other. If any member tried to express an independent thought, the others laughed at him. If any member talked, for example, about getting training in computers to find a good job some day, he was told to forget it; he was too dumb. Besides, he wouldn't stick it out. All the jokes were put-downs, making fun of each other."

The social worker decided to set up a plan to help these boys become resilient and especially to develop identity as individuals, not just as a group. She began with promoting trust, that basic building block of resilience. She encouraged them to trust her by always showing up exactly where and when she said she would. They learned to rely on her word. She showed trust in them by sharing thoughts, risking being made fun of. She showed no fear, smiled at them, and frequently asked for advice on how she could best help them. She was seen as trustworthy. Then she added the promotion of respect—respect for self and respect for others. One example of her technique involved pointing out something a member did—he had told a member of the gang to stop pushing another, smaller member—and showing respect for him through body language (looking straight at him) as well as verbally: "You know, I really respect you for what you did. And I see you have respect for others." The gang member thought about this for a while and then said, "That's cool."

She continued in this way with other resilience factors until she was satisfied that each one had become part of the identity of each member. She said one of the hardest resilience factors to promote was, "I am responsible for my own behavior and accept the consequences." But this process works. The social worker drew on many resilience factors to be able to do this work. Can you determine which ones she used?

# Risk-Taking

Risk-taking is especially attractive in the teens. There is new and increasingly growing freedom, the awareness of greater autonomy, and the seductiveness of feeling invincible. These things, along with hormones kicking in and higher mental processes emerging, such as the ability to reason critically, all add to the joy of being young. Creativity, new ventures, and new solutions to old problems can emerge with few inhibitions. As a result, teens can face adversities with less baggage than adults. One fifteen-year-old leads a campaign to have seat belts required in all school buses. Another eighteen-year-old leads a campaign to rebuild her dangerously old school. A seventeen-year-old organizes community dances in a community where gangs threaten to draw youths into their ranks. Talk about taking on the system! How many adults are good at that? You have to be prepared if you are going to take the risk of challenging the system. You must gather all the information you can, study all the available options, and know when to make your moves.

Did you ever take on the system, alone or with friends? What did you do? Were you successful? Did you involve others? What sorts of responses did you get? How did you feel about what you were doing? How do you feel about it now? Most importantly, how did the experience influence your sense of who you are—your identity?

Temperament is also a critical part of risk-taking. Some teens simply need more excitement and stimulation than others. They get bored easily, are indifferent to the consequences of their actions, believe themselves to be in less danger than others, and are more likely to try something most people would see as foolish. These teens are often not prepared to deal with experiences of adversity. They could benefit from learning to plan ahead and acquiring calming self-talk techniques. How did you fit in where temperament was concerned? Were you easily challenged to action? How did you calm yourself? Do you still have a problem with keeping calm? Do you react too quickly, before you even understand what has happened? You can practice calming yourself by taking a breather, going to a quiet place for a while. If you tend to react before you think, you can practice saying nothing—absolutely nothing—until you have time to process what has happened. Don't be afraid to ask for a "time-out"—adults sometimes need them, too!

## Adversities Common to Teens

There are four common adversities that confront teens (and very likely confronted you). With resilience, these can be dealt with:

1. feeling unconnected to family, school, and the community;

2. engaging in self-destructive activities;

3. having few social- and problem-solving skills; and

4. having no dreams or goals for the future.

The first adversity can be dealt with through maintaining family ties. Let's take a closer look at that.

Teens are attracted to the idea of breaking family ties so that they'll have more freedom and can listen to their peers instead. But teens should be made aware that they can maintain these important ties *and* make changes in their relationships with family members. Here are some things they can do:

- help the family understand their new need for more privacy;

- talk with the family about their expectation that their ideas will be taken more seriously; and

- express their desire to negotiate some of the house rules, particularly those involving their behavior.

If you did not maintain family ties in your teens, you might have lost the basic loving, trusting relationships you need so much to rely on when you are facing adversities today. Family members are there for you. They accept you without limits. They love you. You will not likely have anyone else who can meet their level of love. Now, it may be that your family was so dysfunctional that you had to sever ties. If that was truly necessary, then you need to plan for what you will do now to find a stable, loving, trusting relationship. Everyone needs this to live and deal with adversities. People who love you can help you face an adversity and recover from its effects.

The second adversity from the above list can be dealt with by coming to terms with the tendency to get involved in self-destructive activities. Part of this is examining the reasons for engaging in such activities in the first place.

Teens crave and need excitement and new experiences. That is part of being a teen. But sometimes this behavior becomes self-destructive, which affects the teen's ability to become resilient and deal with the adversities of life. They should seek out friends with whom they can engage in activities that are exciting and fun but not self-destructive, such as drinking and driving, getting addicted to drugs, having unprotected sex, or acting out in anger and violence.

An important thing that happens in the teens is the examining of values, morals, and ethics. Because they are increasingly responsible for their own behavior and because there are some unpleasant legal consequences of doing the wrong thing, teens need to take a close look at their values. As youngsters, people tend to adopt the values of their parents out of love and trust, not because they understand the values. But in the teen years, identity is being developed and people suddenly need to reexamine or, better, develop a set of values consistent with the larger society. These values are part of the "I am" resilience factors; they determine integrity and character and help define identity. Let's look at these values from the point of view of a teen who craves excitement:

- Conservation of human life: Does my need for excitement threaten this value? Does it risk harming others or myself? Do I understand the value of human life?

- Property rights: Is my behavior consistent with respect for the property rights of others or am I tempted to steal or destroy property? Do I understand the importance of respecting property rights?

- Legal limits: Does my behavior push the limits of the law? Do I lie to avoid responsibility? Do I use others to break the law with me? Do I understand the importance of legal limits for a society?

- Democratic process: Can I discuss things openly with others or do I have to manipulate and dominate discussions? Do I understand the importance of fair elections, representation, and the power and rights of people as a whole?

The third adversity from the above list can be dealt with by learning to develop good social- and problem-solving skills. These include:

- making friends who know how to challenge others constructively;

- learning how to listen;

- learning how to express anger, disappointment, disagreement, or empathy without becoming belligerent or causing trouble; and

- developing some effective problem-solving skills using higher mental processes.

The higher mental processes developed during the teen years go beyond observable cause and effect. They include inferring a past cause for something happening now:

"Judy doesn't talk to me anymore. What could be the reason? Let's see. Oh, I'll bet it's because I didn't like it when she criticized me for ignoring her when I saw her at the mall the other day. I can't think of anything else that happened. That must be it. I'll try to set things straight. We could talk about both versions of the event and resolve the conflict." This describes an analytic process.

Reflective thinking, also developed during the teen years, involves having a discussion in your head to examine the pros and cons of an action you are considering. Such thinking uses qualifiers such as, "It is true that Joe looks good as a candidate for class president, but is he more interested in the attention he would get than in taking strong positions on issues we are concerned about?" Reflective thinking about Joe as president would also include thinking about his behavior and predicting how he will behave when dealing with the problems the school faces, and inferring from his past and present behavior what alternative actions might be expected. How has he handled conflicts in the past? Does he listen to people?

When people don't develop problem-solving skills or learn to use their higher mental processes, they fall victim to someone else's skills. They lose their autonomy/independence, they lose their initiative, they lose the skills of industry, and they lose trust in themselves.

The final adversity from the above list can be dealt with by learning how to plan for life. Teens need to plan not only for tomorrow, but for the long term. They should be encouraged to ask themselves the following questions:

- What are my options?

- Who can help me with my planning?

- Am I reading about different careers and making decisions on what will be needed for a chosen path?

- What are my plans for marriage?

That last question is a complex one, because the teen years are the years that people become sexually mature. Teens develop a strong sex drive along with accompanying sexual tensions, and their identity is involved in the sexually related decisions they make. Are they attracted to the opposite sex or the same sex? Do they manage their behavior to prevent unnecessary risks? Do they respect the other person's sexual limits? Making plans for the future, developing the skills necessary to carry out those plans, and engaging in critical and reflective thinking all help teens deal with sexual tensions and interests. If they do not plan for the future, they lose the ability to determine what it will be. They will likely become dependent on what is available at the moment—perhaps anything will do. At that point they've lost control of the ability to make the choices that can meet their future goals. They have lost their identity and no longer know how to deal with the adversities that are bound to come.

## Summing Up Your Building Blocks of Resilience

Now that you've taken a close look at each of the five building blocks of resilience, this is a good time to reflect on how they sum up in your life. For each of these building blocks of resilience, assess yourself on a scale of 1 to 10, with 10 representing "very highly developed within me." Jot the number down in the space provided after each one.

## Trust

Do you trust others with your life, your needs, and your feelings? Do you trust yourself—your abilities, your actions, and your future? Have you identified the problems you might have had early in your life in the development of your trust? If so, have you been able to make any changes in your life that allow you to have more trusting relationships? How do you assess yourself now, using the scale of 1 to 10?

_____

## Autonomy

To what extent do you realize you are a separate person? Did you identify and learn about obstacles early in your life that hindered your developing autonomy? If so, have you been able to change anything so that your autonomy can be strengthened? Have you taken any steps to promote more autonomy in yourself? How do you assess yourself now, using the scale of 1 to 10?

_____

## Initiative

How much interest do you have in starting new things? Have you learned about what enhanced or impeded the development of your initiative earlier in your life? If so, have you done something about it? Have you made some changes? How do you assess yourself now, using the scale of 1 to 10?

_____

## Industry

To what degree do you have mastery of your professional skills and social skills? Were you able to identify any obstacles to the promotion of your industry? If so, have you made some changes so that your industry can be developed further? Has anyone helped you? Do you need to do more? How do you assess yourself now, using the scale of 1 to 10?

_____

## *Identity*

Do you have a firm sense of who you are? Did you learn more about your identity and the obstacles that interfered with its development? Have you taken some action to increase your sense of identity? Has someone helped you? How do you assess yourself now, using the scale of 1 to 10?

You are now ready to use these five basic building blocks, in connection with the related "I have," "I am," and "I can" resilience factors, to face, overcome, and be strengthened by or transformed by experiences of adversity. Have you been integrating these ideas as you were reading? Can you apply them to a situation of adversity you experienced? Have you tried?

The next section of this book provides information about applying these components of resilience to different settings, including common adversities, disastrous adversities, and life-span experiences of adversity. You will learn about ways to promote your own resilience as well as that of those you care about.

Now, assess your resilience quotient again. Has your quotient increased? Which areas still need work?

Resilience on _____ (fill in the date) = _____

Read each of the following statements, and think about how much each one describes you. Then write down a number from 1 to 10, with 10 representing "describes me the most." Then add the score numbers for all twenty-one statements: that total is your resilience quotient today.

### I Have

1. One or more persons within my family I can trust and who love me without reservation.

2. One or more persons outside my family I can trust without reservation.

3. Limits to my behavior.

4. People who encourage me to be independent.

5. Good role models.

6. Access to health, education, and the social and security services I need.

7. A stable family and community.

## I Am

1. A person most people like.

2. Generally calm and good-natured.

3. An achiever who plans for the future.

4. A person who respects myself and others.

5. Empathic and caring of others.

6. Responsible for my own behavior and accepting of the consequences.

7. A confident, optimistic, hopeful person.

## I Can

1. Generate new ideas or new ways to do things.

2. Stay with a task until it is finished.

3. See the humor in life and use it to reduce tensions.

4. Express thoughts and feelings in communication with others.

5. Solve problems in various settings—academic, job-related, personal, and social.

6. Manage my behavior—feelings, impulses, acting-out.

7. Reach out for help when I need it.

# PART TWO

---

## Tapping Your Inner Strength in Everyday Life

# 6

## Resilience and Illness

Home was the first institution where you were vulnerable and school was the second; health-related services is the third. What do I mean by that? Well, you are not very vulnerable when you grocery shop, go to the post office, or buy clothes. If you do not like the way you are treated, you just walk out. But where your health is concerned, you are extremely vulnerable. When you are ill, when you need medication, when you need an operation, you may be vulnerable at a basic survival level. Do you avoid going to doctors? Do you deny pain or ignore symptoms? If you do go, do you resent being a guinea pig as medications are adjusted to your reactions, including some dangerous side effects? Health problems are, of course, an adversity most of us have to deal with at some point in our lives.

When you are depressed, your emotional and social well-being—your happiness—is vulnerable. Do you tell yourself to stop moping and cheer up? Do you blame yourself or the other people involved in your marital or interpersonal relationship problems? What makes you resist or seek help? If you do seek help, do you resent the probing into your past, the labels put on your condition, and/or the feeling that you've initiated a dependency-based relationship? These responses will not promote your resilience or help you deal with the adversity affecting your mental health. Only resilience provides you with the inner strengths and the interpersonal and problem-solving skills to face and overcome the adversity, rather than blaming, avoiding, and resenting.

# Who Is in Control of Your Health?

This is an exciting time because health services are now incorporating resilience factors into their services. They do not always use that term, but the practices it stands for are now becoming understood. Former U.S. Surgeon General C. Everett Koop, a confrontational, stand-on-your-own-feet, protect-yourself kind of guy, tells people how to manage their doctors rather than the other way around. He tells people to know their own bodies, to write out questions they want answered during their appointment with their doctor, to be their own advocate and seek second opinions, to trust their intuition, and to follow directions they agree to. From a resilience perspective, he is promoting independence, responsibility, communication, and problem-solving. He encourages people to be independent of outside control, to give up the dependency relationship with doctors. He encourages people to be responsible for their own health conditions and needs and to give up irresponsible behaviors that cause many health problems. He encourages people to acquire more knowledge about their health problem, to give up passivity and denial. He urges people to communicate their concerns about their health, ask questions and express feelings, and give up submission and ignorance. All of these things empower the patient—you. Resilience and empowerment make a great team.

Another interesting change is the fact that the Veterans Health Administration, in early 1999, added a fifth vital sign to the four major health indicators: pulse, temperature, respiration, and blood pressure. The fifth is pain. This means that pain is now seen as critical to your health; patients no longer have to assume they must bear the pain that accompanies so many illnesses. Of course, pain is a subjective feeling, not a measurable condition—and involving feelings has been contrary to medical science, where objectivity and measurement reign. The fact that pain is now recognized, without measurement but with just the simple question "Are you experiencing pain?" is a dramatic change. Subjective experiences are now accepted, which suggests to a patient some expression of empathy and caring, which as you know is one of the resilience factors. Empathy and caring are important to your health. I wonder how fast this new health indicator will be adopted by other providers of health services. There is also growing awareness of the role of fatigue as a side effect of an operation or medication. I have not seen any agency or organization formally adopt fatigue as a major interest, but it is frequently mentioned on TV shows.

## Conflicts with Health Care Providers

In spite of the growing awareness of the importance of subjective measures of health conditions, a great many providers of health care are having difficulty accepting some of the recent thinking. As you become more independent, more responsible, engage in more communication, and participate more in problem-solving, you will inevitably have conflicts with health professionals. The old way of thinking is deep-seated: These people have more knowledge than you. They have the authority and status society has given them. They are the professionals; you are an amateur. But, as you promote your own resilience, you will learn to be more in charge of what happens to you. So, conflicts will occur.

Here are four major conflicts clients have had with providers of health care. As you read these, place a check mark next to the ones you have experienced:

1. Objective (cure-oriented) versus subjective (care-oriented) focus on the health problem
   The professional looks at the problem—the adversity—objectively. He or she wants to know what the health problem is and what the symptoms are. The condition is considered independent of the person. This model stems from the medical model: diagnose and treat only the illness. The patient as an individual is somewhat lost in this formula. You, however, are more likely to look at the problem—the adversity—subjectively. You probably ask yourself questions such as, "Am I in serious trouble? Will I be able to do the things I want to? How long will this condition last? What is the prognosis? Will this affect my job, my loved ones?" This way of thinking is care-oriented, while the other is cure-oriented.

2. Verbal versus nonverbal behavior
   The professional focuses on the language of the profession: diagnosis, labels, medication, and directives. The client focuses on nonverbal behavior: attitudes, attention, empathy, acceptance, and concern. The attitudes of some providers suggest distance from the client at best or, at worst, even blaming the client for the condition. Many clients report having been scolded. Attitudes and feelings communicate directly to the client and often determine what the client will do about advice or even about returning for treatment. The client is the vulnerable one in health-related services and needs to feel safe in a caring, trusting relationship with the provider. Health care providers have not only been taught to keep a professional distance, but many are reluctant to become involved with the patient as a person. They fear that the emotions of

empathy and caring will blind them to the objectivity needed for determining the health condition.

3. Controlling behavior

The professional focuses on the management of the client to follow procedures of the examination, and is especially concerned about compliance to recommendations and medications. In this scenario, the authority of the service provider is to be accepted without time for explanations. But the client wants to be seen as a participant in decision making and does not want to feel controlled. The client may accept the controlling behavior because of lack of an alternative, but the resentment is there and may show up in a failure to take medication or keep appointments.

4. Medical versus everyday language

The professional uses medical language that has become as ordinary to him or her as regular conversation, without seeming to care that the specialized meaning is usually lost on the client and needs defining. Doctors don't always explain in everyday language what the medications do or what people need to know about them. Clients need everyday language to be used to explain the condition, the prognosis, and the path to restored health.

How many check marks did you make for the four conflicts listed above? What does this number tell you about the experiences with health-related services you've received? Pick one of your conflicts to examine in terms of resilience. What was the experience? Describe it in as much detail as possible in the blank lines below. Ask yourself the following questions:

- What happened?

- What did you do?

- How did you feel?

- What did the provider do?

- How do you think the provider felt?

- How did the situation come out?

With the full description of the event in mind, now focus more on the implications of that event for the promotion of your resilience factors of trusting relationships ("I have"), optimism ("I am"), and communication ("I can"), all of which are needed in your relationship with a provider.

- What did the health care provider do or say that helped strengthen these resilience factors?

- What did you do (what actions did you take and what decisions did you make) as part of that experience that promoted the three resilience factors?

- What did you do (what actions did you take and what decisions did you make) that did not promote the three resilience factors?

- What would you do differently if you could have that experience again?

_____

_____

_____

_____

_____

_____

## *Expectations within a Resilience Framework*

When you go to a professional for health services, you have certain expectations. You want help with your health problem. You want to understand why you feel the way you do. You want to get better. Your expectations may be unrealistic, but they are real to you. What about expectations that are within a resilience framework—your expectations to receive more empathy, more caring, better communication, and greater involvement in decision making? These are equally real; in fact, you have a right to these things.

One university program (F. Edward Hebert School of Medicine) trains medical students to honor such expectations within a resilience framework. The program involves parents who provide their point of view on the needs of their children and of their families. The parents also are quite frank in telling the medical students what they need to do and what is missing in their interactions with parents. They are especially critical when the students fall into the common practice of talking to a parent about the child as though the child were not there and can't hear everything. Often, children with special needs are presumed not to understand what is going on.

One mother who was part of the program provided a parent's point of view of what expectations she had for her seven-year-old son, who is developmentally delayed and autistic. She was familiar with the resilience paradigm "I have," "I am," "I can." She cleverly and endearingly wrote from the child's perspective:

## I Have

- Those who truly care about my educational and personal needs.

- My educator's willingness to respect and listen to those that know me best and who are trying to advocate for me.

- Creative problem-solvers who will develop a truly individualized program to help me succeed to my fullest possible potential.

- A cooperative teaching team who will respectfully work together with each other and my caregivers to help me be the best I can be.

## I Am

- A mountain of untapped potential waiting to be discovered.

- A unique individual who has abilities, feelings, hopes, dreams, and a spirit.

- Special to my family and others who have entrusted me to you for my days.

- An important part of our classroom—not only to be taught, but to give to others and teach them things about life they might never learn from a book.

- Trusting in you to treat me as you would your own child.

## I Can

- Be happy and confident.

- Love school and the excitement of learning new things.

- Be an integral part of our educational community.

- Develop the self-esteem from daily accomplishments that I can take with me through life.

- Participate in most things with my classmates and develop friendships because I am likable.

- Challenge myself and achieve what success means to me.

- Help problem-solve for myself, yet count on my educational role models to help me out if I need it.

- Develop attitudes, strengths, abilities, and character that will help me contribute to the world around me for the rest of my life.

The value of this report is not only in the way the mother absorbed the resilience categories, but how she mixed and blended the resilience factors in each category. She is, of course, intuitively correct. Resilience factors do overlap, they do work in dynamic inter-action, they do begin to blend. They are interdependent.

# Health Problems and Resilience

Health problems can transform people just as other adversities have been found to do. Anyone who has a serious health condition them-selves or is involved with someone else who has one can be trans-formed by the adversity. One medical student in the aforementioned program made his decision to become a pediatrician after he and his wife experienced this heartbreaking experience of adversity:

> My wife and I received exciting news one day that we were expecting twins! This news came as quite a shock since we were not planning for more children. You see, a year earlier we were expecting the delivery of our second daughter when, for unknown reasons, complications arose and we delivered a stillborn child. The sadness and emotional tur-moil we endured was overwhelming, causing great strain on our personal and social lives. Through much anguish and guilt, we searched for answers to this unfortunate inci-dent. The health services were not very helpful in this pur-suit. It was only a year later, after much insistence and persistence, that we were given help. We learned that my wife suffered from a rare form of lupus. So the joy of the news of twins, was, of course, dampened by the knowledge of a complicated pregnancy.
>
> Although every precaution was taken to bring the pregnancy to term, at twenty-three weeks premature infants were delivered. Surgeries and seizures plagued the twins. As a second-year medical student I understood the medical terminology and the complications, but as a parent I was

lost in the milieu of uncertainty and stress. For five months we made the neonatal intensive care unit our second home, suffering through many setbacks and close bouts with death. Although it's difficult to understand, we found joy and strength in this experience. Each second was precious and each achievement momentous. Our hearts filled with pride and tears flowed with joy at Connor's smile and Kennedy's twinkling eyes.

They did not make it. But their very existence changed our lives forever and touched each member of the health care team. Our neonatologist, once viewed as our primary physician, became friend and confidant, and integrated our every concern into health care planning and delivery. The wonderful nurses we encountered took on the role of surrogates in our absence and reveled in each accomplishment the twins achieved as if they were their own.

What was the role of resilience in this tragedy? The student and his wife had confronted a previous experience of adversity when they had a stillborn daughter a year earlier. They had been through a tragedy and learned from it as they worked through the impact of the tragedy on their relationship. Then, they faced the lack of helpfulness from the health services and persisted in seeking answers to their problem. They finally learned the cause of the tragedy. They had learned enough about living through tragedy—and how to deal with it—to actually be excited about the news of twins. The birth of the twins brought both tragedy and joy. They were not going to make it, but they gave their parents joy every day they lived; their every response was shared by the parents with joy. When the twins died, the parents both realized how important it was for the father to become a pediatrician, specializing in working with children with special needs. This was the transformation.

## A Health Care Provider's Perspective

Both the providers and the clients of services are involved in resilience, and both can face the shared adversities and become stronger as a result. In this way the use of resilience factors promotes resilience in both the providers and the clients of services. After all, resilience does not develop in just one direction. All participants dealing with an adversity are going to be affected by the role of resilience. In what way can providers promote resilience? Put yourself in the provider's shoes for a moment. Maybe you will feel some empathy for him or her!

In each encounter between a provider of services and a client, the provider can promote resilience by using resilience factors from "I have." These involve the provision of good services and assurance to the client of a trusting relationship. The provider can promote his or her own resilience by having access to the best possible services available to draw on, and trust in their quality.

The provider also promotes the resilience of the client by using resilience factors from "I am." This is done by helping the client be emotionally and personally strong enough to overcome the adversity. One way is to listen for the feelings the client expresses. Once a feeling is heard, the provider can label it: "You seem angry," or "You seem frustrated. Can I help?" Offering reassurances is important, as is giving time for the client to express his or her feelings. Empathy and caring are the emotions clients most want to see in the providers. The provider promotes his or her own resilience by becoming increasingly confident and comfortable in dealing with the health problems of clients, recognizing their emotional needs as well as their health needs.

The provider also promotes the resilience of the client by using resilience factors from "I can." These include encouraging the client to communicate about the adversity and participating in dealing with the adversity, such as suggesting some solutions. The provider promotes his or her own resilience by developing the interpersonal skills needed to deal effectively with both the client and the other providers also involved with the client.

You can decide where you can incorporate resilience into your interactions with health providers. You may even decide it would be useful to tell the provider what you would find helpful with your health problem in terms of resilience factors. You don't need to use the term "resilience factors," of course. Just explain what would be helpful to you. "It would be helpful to me if you would clarify what you mean by those medical terms." "I need to tell you how I feel about what is happening because I am very upset." "Thank you for listening to my concerns. I appreciate your time." "I need to know what side effects I should be looking for in this medication and what I should do about them."

## Becca's Story

Here is a nice example of a resilience-promoting environment during a major adversity. Becca had a five-year battle with brain cancer. She had surgery, radiation, and gene therapy, and was hoping to avoid chemotherapy. But the brain tumor was growing again. The pediatric cancer specialist went over the options with the parents and cautioned them that the chance of anything curing her at this point was diminishing, but he said that chemotherapy would help reduce Becca's chronic headaches and fatigue, occasional brief spells of dizziness, and double vision. He noted, however, that the decision to undertake chemo must be a personal decision, not one he should make for them.

The parents wanted to discuss the options alone before they talked with Becca. Unfortunately, Becca saw that her mother had been crying and asked about it, so her mother, feeling Becca deserved an answer, told her the truth. There was no reaction from Becca. The parents tried to ease Becca past her mental block against chemo, as that was the only option left. They did not succeed, but a neurologist did. He explained that one of the hardest things for a cancer patient was to consider another tough treatment when she was feeling good. He suggested a particular chemo and she wanted to know if she would lose her hair. He said she probably would, but that it would grow back when the treatment stopped. He explained how the chemo would work and he explained the dangers attached to it.

Becca was a typical teenager and wanted to behave as one—she wanted to be accepted and do what her friends do. She wanted to be at school and be part of the scene there. Her parents and school personnel agreed on a special curriculum for Becca that allowed her to carry only half a schedule. A teacher who was also Becca's on-campus guardian worked with Becca and the family to adapt to Becca's changing needs. For example, as she lost her ability to remember things she was learning through hearing, she was taught through visual images.

Becca tried to be as normal as possible and to be accepted. She refused offers of special trips or outings by her parents because she just wanted to be treated as a normal kid. Her close friend said that Becca was one of the bravest people she had met. Becca shared her feelings with her friend, and when the friend realized something was wrong because Becca seemed especially upset, she took Becca to the counselor. When Becca cried about taking the chemo, her friend said it was okay to be scared. The pediatric cancer specialist talked to her about day-to-day concerns related to the chemo treatment, and told her to keep up her energy by eating whatever appealed to her. He also talked about ways to deal with her hair if it began to fall out. He suggested a shorter hair style that made use of wigs or scarves. Becca's sister said she would shave off her own hair if Becca's came out, and the younger brother said his was already so short it was like he'd be bald, too. The entire family had been with her during the chemo sessions.

Becca's teacher, who knew she loved young children and was aware that she could not take difficult subjects, got her into a pre-school three days a week to acquire credits in life skills at the high school. The children adored her.

Each summer for four years, Becca had attended Camp Fantastic for one week. The children who attend are also ill with some condition, but the camp leaders are used to seeing kids, not diseases. For one week the kids don't have to explain anything to anybody. The goal of the camp is to get the kids who are fighting for their lives to say, "I can do this!"

Let's look at how resilience was promoted and applied in the family as it dealt with the severe health problems Becca faced.

### I Have Trusting Relationships

The love and trust in the family were always there for each member and there was never any wavering in its consistency. Becca could trust her parents to be honest with her, and they were—when she asked her mother why she had been crying, the mother did not try to conceal what she had just learned from the doctor. The brother and sister were also supportive, and did an especially endearing thing when they talked about what they would do with their own hair, as it became clear Becca would lose hers. The doctors, nurses, and teachers never betrayed or abused the trust the family placed in them. Teachers changed the curriculum for Becca as her condition worsened, knowing she wanted to stay in school and be with her peers. Her doctor expressed empathy over her fears about losing her hair but he did not attempt to gloss over the fact that she would probably lose it.

### I Have Access to Services

The family had access to the best services and the resources to pay for them. This is not always the case, but you can see how effective such access is for people facing serious adversities. She had a teacher who was willing to be quite flexible about Becca's course of study, not only in the way she could learn (visually, with less focus on hearing) but also in what she could learn (arranging school credits through preschool work). The opportunity to attend Camp Fantastic was especially helpful.

### I Have a Stable Family

The family was constant in its support of Becca and made changes as her condition required. Becca knew her family was there for her. Her parents offered special trips or outings, and allowed

Becca the opportunity to decide for herself whether or not she needed those things. The entire family had been with her during the chemo sessions.

### I Am a Person Most People Like

Becca had many friends and even the children she taught liked her. She had a best friend, but was liked by her peer group as well. It did not matter that she was limited in what she could do. She was accepted. Her best friend liked her so much she kept an eye on her emotional state and when Becca seemed especially upset, she even took her to the school counselor to make sure she'd be okay.

### I Am Generally Good-Natured

Becca had the ability to distance herself from some of the more distressing aspects of her increasingly serious health condition. She kept active and attempted to focus on things she could do and let go of the things she could not do. Her strong desire to perform as much school work as she could, even if it meant just half a schedule, is a good example of this.

### I Can Stay with a Task

Becca was persistent in her work, whether it was with the young children or in her assignments. She returned to them as soon as she recovered from therapy, and she stayed with them as long as her health permitted.

### I Can Express Thoughts and Feelings in Communication with Others

Becca had an indirect way of communicating with others—she did much of her communicating through the choices she made. She wanted to be like other teens. She wanted a sense of identity. She insisted on being treated like her peers. She did not want special trips or outings.

Have you ever had an experience that involved someone who was living through a life-threatening adversity?

- What was the experience?

- Who was involved?

- What was the life-threatening condition?

- What services were provided?

- Did the service providers demonstrate any of the resilience factors? Which ones?

- Did family members or friends demonstrate any of the resilience factors? Who, and which factors?

- What was your role in the experience?

- Did you demonstrate any of the resilience factors? Which ones?

- Would you suggest ways that the experience could have involved resilience factors for the benefit of all involved? What are they?

_____

_____

_____

_____

_____

_____

_____

## *Keep Your Eyes Open*

As you read the newspaper or magazines or watch TV, begin to look for stories that describe experiences of people's adversities. Use the paradigm "I have," "I am," "I can," and identify the resilience factors used in facing, overcoming, and being strengthened or even transformed by the experience of adversity. Ask yourself what resilience factors were used for "I have"? For "I am"? For "I can"? What was lacking for each of those? Then look at the dynamic interaction of the resilience factors. Finally, ask yourself what would have been a better way to promote or apply resilience in these situations of adversity? What could I have done differently so that the outcome would be more favorable?

# 7

---

# Interpersonal Relationships

A CEO of a large company has been asked to leave. He was very successful in his work and performed wonders for the company, but he also engaged in tyrannical behavior toward subordinates. Fellow workers claimed his management style contributed to a climate of tension and anxiety. They were afraid to disagree with him because he would verbally attack them and humiliate them in front of others. He scolded and shamed people in public as if they were children—he managed by fear. That kind of interpersonal relationship is not accepted anymore.

Authoritarian management was effective for many years. In fact, you may have experienced it yourself. But today we know that people increase their productivity if they feel involved in decision making, are consulted for opinions and ideas, and are treated with respect. The authoritarian model for interpersonal relationships was also common in homes and in school, though now there is a move toward increasingly democratic interpersonal relationships in which each person is seen as part of the functioning of the home, school, and work. Authority exists, of course, but it just isn't absolute.

# Enhancing Interpersonal Skills

Interpersonal relations are crucial to promoting resilience and in dealing with experiences of adversity. Every time you reach out for help, you engage in interpersonal relationships. Every time someone has made you angry or upset, interpersonal relationships were involved. The more skilled you are in your interpersonal relationships, the more easily you are able to deal with adversities. These skills are taught. After they're taught, the reasons for them are learned or figured out, and then they are practiced.

But don't count on the skills being applied all the time. Take road rage, an all-too-common condition in our country. People who have been taught all the proper interpersonal skills suddenly engage in actions that must scare even them. We tailgate dangerously close, and if the car doesn't move fast enough, we honk, curse, or give an unfriendly signal. If we're really mad and want to "teach them a lesson," we get in front of them and brake, scaring the driver and forcing him to slam on the brakes. Now the second driver is angry and in a state of rage. Revenge is needed. All kinds of reasons are given for why this may wind up with a fight, destruction of property, or an arrest. The drivers are frustrated with all the traffic. They are tired from a long day. Work didn't go well and they are unhappy with their jobs. Their cars are capsules and they are disconnected from those outside. There is no room for courtesy. There is no thought of acceptable interpersonal relationships. If you've ever engaged in such behavior, read on.

Interpersonal relationships involve a great deal of communication, but this is not always easy. Earlier in this book, you read about communication at home and in school; now you will examine communication in the broader personal and social settings where you spend your time. Now that you've left your childhood behind, you want more adult ways of communicating your needs, problems, and frustrations. Language is still your major instrument, of course, whether you use it physically, verbally, or emotionally.

## Body Language

Body language is used almost subconsciously. If someone comes to you and shows by his body that he is frightened, confused, and reaching out to you, there is little doubt in your mind that this person really needs help. You look to (and respond to) his body language to validate his words. Think of the way body language is conveyed during a courtroom trial. What is the defendant's body language? Does she sit rigidly or relaxed? Does she look others in the eye or does she evade direct eye contact? Does she seem to be taking the proceedings seriously or is she just doodling? Throughout the day we make decisions about how to interact with people that are dependent on others' body language. Our body language communicates in exactly the same way. Literally where you stand in relation to someone else— how close and what, if anything, is touching—will to some extent determine the outcome of the interaction.

### Active Listening

Body language is especially important when you are listening to someone who wants your attention. It sets the stage for "active listening," a somewhat complex skill. Active listening refers to listening without giving advice, clarifying your understanding of what is being said, picking up the emotional content of the words and labeling them, summarizing the situation, and helping (as appropriate) in a plan of action. Let's look at each of these components in more detail.

- Listening without giving advice
  If you need someone's help and reach out for it, you are expected to specify the help you need. But, in reality, you may really want someone to solve the problem for you, to get you out of the adversity and make it go away. The person in a position to provide help may be tempted to do just that. But such a response would not contribute to the promotion of your resilience and would very likely be resented over time. You need to feel competent, not ineffectual; independent, not dependent; stronger, not weaker; proud, not ashamed.

- Clarifying your understanding of what is being said
  You won't *always* understand what is being said. You may think you understand but aren't quite sure. So it's often a good idea to state back to the person what was said. "Let me make sure I understand you. You said you would meet me at four. Did you mean you would have the materials ready at that time, or did you mean we would work on them together at that time?" Generally, it's a good idea to summarize the main points of what someone has stated and ask if your understanding is correct. People appreciate your paying so much attention to what they are saying.

- Picking up the emotional content of the words and labeling them
  Feelings probably motivate behavior more than thoughts. Many people don't recognize that fact and tend to believe that everything is controlled by thoughts. Even some of our major theorists in the field of human behavior believed (or

believe) not only in the separation of thinking and feeling but in the dominance of thought. Jean Piaget, a prominent philosopher and student of cognitive development, presented the development of cognitive, or thinking, skills in isolation from emotional development. We know better now, and certainly, in the last decade, have gathered sufficient information and experience to recognize the role of emotions and emotional understanding in human behavior.

As the listener, then, you need to pick up the emotional content of what a person is saying to you and what the body language is expressing. You can then ask if you have labeled the feelings correctly. Of course, you can be very wrong about what body language is saying about feelings. Here's an experience I had with my three children in which I tried but was completely off base.

One evening, my children—five-year-old twins and a seven-year-old—were watching the movie *Johnny Appleseed*. It was animated for children and beautifully produced.

Johnny Appleseed's story is great. Here is a man who has found a mission in life, walking around the country and planting apple seeds with the faith that trees will grow. He dies, but even after death, finds he can do the same thing in heaven. He's a happy man.

My children began to sob. Quietly, but they did not stop. I said, "He's fine. He's in heaven and is very happy." They continued to sob. I said, "Really, he is okay and is doing exactly what he wants." They continued to sob.

Now I was becoming worried. What was wrong? What was upsetting them so much? I thought I'd better find out. "Are you crying because he died?" All three heads shook no. "What is it then?" Finally, one of them said, "Because he had to walk so far!" The other two nodded in agreement. They had not said a word among themselves, yet each cried for the same reason. I tried to explain that he did that walking over many, many years and had lots of time to rest in between. That still was not enough to stop their crying. And then I realized that my children connected emotionally with his walking. We lived out in the country and one of the problems was getting the three ready to drive into town for all kinds of appointments: shopping, church, and errands. Even school required being ready for the bus. The common threat we used to get them moving was, "If you aren't ready in time, you will have to walk to town."

As soon as I realized the connection I felt better, and after a few laughs over their interpretation of his walking, we all felt better. I also realized that the threat had roused too many unpleasant feelings. From then on I found different, less distressing, ways to get the kids ready.

- Summarizing the situation and helping (as appropriate) in a plan of action

  When interpersonal relations lead to a plan of action, it is important to summarize what points have been made, clarify what decisions have been made, and state clearly what the plan of action is.

## Verbal Communication

Verbal communication is incredibly difficult. You have more than likely experienced problems at some point in expressing thoughts, feelings, instructions, choices, and rules in a way that others could understand. Words are a major source of misunderstandings because they have different meanings to different people. Sometimes this is because our vocabularies do not include enough words to express exactly what we're feeling. Sometimes the speaker is experiencing such intense feelings that the words just don't come to her. Verbal communication is really dependent on people being calm enough to find the words and express them in understandable ways. Checking with the other person from time to time is a useful way to determine if verbal communication is really going on. When you need help in facing an adversity, the words really need to be there.

### Uses of Words

The words you use in interpersonal relationships not only express the way you think and the values you hold, but also the expectations you have from the relationships. Because you are at risk for rejection, humiliation, misunderstanding, and/or making a fool of yourself, you may join the huge numbers of people who avoid expressing thoughts, values, and expectations. This fear begins in the home when siblings mock what you say by belittling the intent of the words or teasing you about the words you used. Do you have memories of such experiences?

# Emotional Literacy

All interpersonal relationships have an emotional component that, in the final analysis, either keeps the relationship going or destroys it. If that emotional component is negative, the relationship will break down or will become hostile, distrustful, and/or destructive. Ask any couple breaking up.

It is difficult to believe, but only in the last decade have human behaviorists seriously considered the role that emotions play in our thinking, decision making, and in our behavior. Again, emotions cannot be dissociated from thinking. The interaction is profound: "I don't like my job. I failed to get the account I wanted. I don't like myself for failing." "I don't like my teacher. He keeps scolding me for not doing my homework. I don't like my teacher for scolding me. I don't like school because I don't like my teacher because he keeps scolding me for not doing my homework. I don't understand the homework because I don't know how to do those kinds of problems and I can't admit that. I don't like myself because I don't understand the work. I am a failure."

You can greatly benefit from identifying your feelings, labeling them, talking about them, understanding their role in your life, and changing them as appropriate. Practice naming your emotions: I feel . . . sad, concerned, angry, frightened, belittled, ignored, controlled, encouraged, criticized, protected, manipulated, rejected, approved, accepted, loved, good, or bad. In this way you are able to talk about your feelings, and when you can talk abut them you are able to do many things that promote your interpersonal relationships. These include:

- Understanding your emotional responses
  "I sure am afraid to go into this interview. I feel as if I am not ready to answer all their questions, especially if they ask about why I left the last job. How can I tell about that embarrassing incident when I was tricked into giving incorrect information? How can I tell about everything that led up to my needing to find a new job?"

  Once you recognize your fear, you can decide that it may be worse to try to explain it than to wait to see if it comes up in the interview. Then you can practice some answers that are truthful and do not hurt others, and then go in for the interview. Knowing the reason for your fear helps you manage it better.

- Managing emotionally impulsive and destructive behavior
  When you know your emotions, have words for them, and recognize when you are feeling them, you are able to think about them and learn how to manage them. You know that you react very strongly with annoyance when a certain relative begins to talk about politics. Your views are diametrically opposed and the discussions inevitably lead to one of you walking out in disgust. Knowing this, you can suggest you talk about something else. You can refuse to respond to the relative. You can tell the relative you feel emotional pain as a result of the conversations and you don't feel it's worth it.

Anger Management, a program I helped develop, is organized around the acronym RETHINK to address anger in interpersonal relationships, especially unresolved anger. Your unresolved anger blocks your understanding of what is going on in your interpersonal relationships and also affects the way you deal with adversities. First, it prevents you from understanding an adversity someone else is facing. Second, it blocks your own capacity to deal successfully with adversity. If anger is dominating your thinking and feeling, you are handicapped: your unresolved anger is in the way of any resolution. Each letter of the RETHINK acronym is used to organize thoughts and actions that lead to anger management in interpersonal relationships. As you read and answer the questions, place a check mark next to those skills you think you already have, and place an X next to the items you do not have or need to work on.

Recognize when you are feeling angry.

What are you thinking when you are angry? Who is angry, you or the other person? What is the cause of your anger? What is the cause of the other person's anger? Being able to recognize what is making you angry is critical to clarifying the issue causing the anger. It also helps you separate real causes from the common practice of using anger as a cover-up for other feelings such as fear, shame, stress, fatigue, or embarrassment.

Empathize with the person making you angry.

What do you think the other person is feeling, thinking, and experiencing? Can you remember having the same feelings? Can you step back during an anger attack and then empathize by stepping into the other person's shoes? Can you think of a few reasons the person did what he did—besides intentionally wanting to hurt you?

Think about your own thoughts that make you angry.

Can you think about the same situation in a different way? Can you find some humor in it? What can you tell yourself to change the way you feel?

What else can you tell yourself so you don't magnify your feelings of anger?

Hear what the other person is saying.

Can you hear the other person's words as well as the feelings behind them? Can you use your listening skills to determine what the other person is upset or worried about? Can you let the person know that you understand where he or she is coming from by using your body language? Can you tell the person in words that you know he or she is angry, upset, hurt, scared, or frightened?

Integrate expressions of anger with expressions of love and respect.

Can you get something off your chest without upsetting the other person? Do you recognize that the tone of your voice affects a conversation involving anger? Do you know how a gentle touch on the shoulder or hand affects a conversation involving anger? Can you tell the person you are angry but that the relationship is intact; there is simply a problem you both need to deal with?

Notice what your body feels like when you are angry.

What is your heart doing when you are angry? What does your neck feel like when you are angry? What does your head feel like when you are angry? Do you know how to relax your body? Do you know that it is okay to walk away when someone else is losing control?

Keep the conversation in the present.

Do you know how to avoid opening old wounds? Do you know how to forgive and forget? Do you know what it means to "pick your battles carefully"? Do you know how to control yourself so you don't bring up hurts and problems that were left unresolved in the past?

Think of an experience you had that involved anger. Ask yourself the following questions.

- What happened?

- What did you do?

- How did you feel, especially with regard to your feelings of anger?

- What did the other person do in response?

- How do you think that person felt, especially with regard to the feelings of anger?

- How did the situation come out?

With that full description of the event in mind, now focus more on the implications of that event for your management of anger in interpersonal relationships.

- What happened in the experience that enhanced your ability to manage your anger? What actions did you take? What decisions did you make? What did you learn?

- What happened in the experience that had a negative impact on your ability to manage your anger? What actions did you take? What decisions did you make? What did you learn?

_____

_____

_____

_____

## *Expanding Your Emotional Vocabulary*

Try expanding your repertoire of emotions or, at least, try to recognize and label your emotions. One useful exercise is marking words in books (biographies are good for this) or magazines that identify and define emotions. The newspaper is not a bad place to look, either. News analyses or stories will be the best route; factual news tends to use simple, basic words of emotion. "This team killed that team; this politician creamed that one."

Another exercise you will find useful is to label all the feelings you now have or recognize. You might organize them into groups: positive and negative, helpful and harmful, happy and sad, optimistic and pessimistic, joyful and depressed. In what direction do your emotions tend to lean? More toward positive feelings or more toward negative feelings? You *can* change the direction. Feelings are not fixed; they can change quite easily. They do all the time.

Still another activity you might want to engage in is this: make note of the emotional words you use in relationship to others, especially when you talk about them. What is the balance between words of acceptance and caring versus words of criticism and disapproval? The kinds of words you use when you are talking about someone not present are often seen as an expression of your values and attitudes. If the words are negative or critical, they communicate to the listener to beware of you because you may do the same thing to them when they are not present. Trust is broken and the interpersonal relationships are more restricted—yet these relationships are so critical in dealing with adversities.

# Different Settings

Interpersonal relationships change in different settings, too. When you are at home, your interpersonal relationships are informal and intimate. You use language—physical, verbal, and emotional—in very different ways and with very specific meanings. You say and do what you want and expect to be understood and accepted. You are generally uninhibited. But when you bring those same informal, intimate behaviors out in public you get into trouble. Children have an especially difficult time understanding the line between the end of intimacy and the beginning of increasing formality.

In the workplace, the lines between formal/informal and intimate/interpersonal relationships are drawn by custom or by the particular culture that develops over time in a company. The computer industry brought in a whole new style of workplace—informal, casual, friendly, almost intimate, with few lines separating "boss" from "bossed." Generally speaking, there is currently a social trend in our country toward the informal. When limits are set, they are done so increasingly by the individual persons involved in the interaction rather than by external rules. A college professor is called by his first name in class and accepts that as a sign of student comfort. Another professor at the same college recoils at the intimacy and states quite clearly how she is to be addressed. How do you feel about kids calling their mother or father by their first names?

You tend to set limits as you share or discuss events and feelings. This is important when you need help in facing an adversity or are helping someone else. How personal do you get in your questions? How much do you share? Perhaps you share more than you intended and have serious regrets and misgivings later. (Will he tell others what I said? Will he use it against me later? Do I have to be especially nice to him now because I have revealed too much?) It is not easy to determine limits of interpersonal relations, but there are few adversities you face that do *not* involve interpersonal relationships. The way you interact with people, the words you use, the level of intimacy you take—all are inclined to influence what kind of help you get. This may seem unfair, but think about it. If someone treats you in a way you are uncomfortable with, you are less willing to respond to his request for help. If you use language that is too intimate, you may find people avoiding you. Make note of what kinds of interpersonal relationships are appropriate in different settings. Being aware will make you more likely to get help when you need it.

## Compassion

Compassion combines the recognition of the pain of someone else or yourself with the desire to do something that shows your caring for the welfare of that person or yourself. Recognizing and feeling the pain is an act of empathy. Being motivated to do something about the pain brings in altruism, and both define compassion. These are resilience factors and are inherent in facing, overcoming, and being strengthened or transformed by experiences of adversity. As we feel the pain of someone else facing an experience of adversity we are in a position to promote their resilience and strengthen our own. You cannot help someone else deal with an adversity without becoming more resilient yourself. You learn from their experience, you know what feelings need to be shared, you know what is important and what needs to be ignored. You are more empowered to deal with your next experience of adversity.

## Expressing Compassion

Compassionate people hold a basic set of values about others that guides the way as they express their compassion. Compassionate people care about what happens to you because they care about you as a human being. They see you as a worthwhile, even sacred individual, as is everyone. Their behavior reflects that belief in your worthiness. Their skills in interpersonal relationships express that belief.

Compassionate people are recognizable by the way they behave. You don't have to get to know them too well to determine they are compassionate—their behavior shouts it. You intuitively reach out for them, trust them, and know they will help you. The skills of compassion are recognizable. How many of these skills do you have?

1. Making friends easily
   The compassionate person is friendly. He is not afraid of people and can reach out to them. He is open to becoming a friend if that seems to be a good idea, and is not defensive or shy in the sense that he fears rejection by others. The compassionate person assumes acceptance.

2. Feeling empathy when something unpleasant happens to someone
   The compassionate person is empathic. He can feel, at least for an instant, the pain someone is going through when an adversity has occurred. He shows concern by saying some words of comfort or understanding and offers help, if it is desired.

3. Honest about reactions
   The compassionate person talks to others when they do something that upsets her. She does not hold a grudge or wait to get even. She can express what is bothering her about the other's behavior, with the intent of it changing so the relationship can continue.

4. Managing negative emotions
   The compassionate person knows that others are distressed by her anger, fear, or desire for revenge. She seeks discussion,

negotiation, and resolution of problems causing strong negative emotions. The goal is to enhance relationships, not destroy them.

5. Expecting fairness

The compassionate person assumes fairness in relationships and is quite willing to address any perceived violation of fairness. Violations would include unfair rules and regulations, unfair grading, unfair promotions, unfair treatment of family members, and other acts that seem unfair when measured by concepts of equity and equality. The questioning would be done without rancor or accusation. Anger may, however, be expressed and explained.

6. Demonstrating affection

The compassionate person is not afraid to show affection for others. He is quite willing to hug someone or tell the other person how he feels about them. Some people do not want physical contact, so they can be told in words and smiles that they are liked.

7. Listening

The compassionate person listens to those who approach him. He gives attention, responses, and respect to the person being listened to. He does not try to tell the person what to do.

8. Accepting compliments and praise from others

The compassionate person is able to accept approval from others without belittling it with comments such as, "Oh, I didn't do anything special," or "I don't deserve this praise. Others did much more." Compassionate people tend to praise others quite often, but they sometimes have difficulty accepting similar appreciation.

9. Initiating conversations

The compassionate person is willing to start a conversation with someone else or with a group in order to show a friendly recognition of others. How many times have you been in an elevator where no one says a word? You can feel the tension or, worse, the indifference as the floors go by.

10. Asking for help

A compassionate person trusts others enough to feel free to ask for help when she needs it. She has built a network of supports so that she does not feel alone or abandoned when an experience of adversity occurs. She approaches others with respect and clear need, and her attitude says she expects them to help because she knows others are good human beings, too.

- Which of these ten skills of compassion do you have now?

- Which ones do you want to improve? How will you do that?

- Which ones don't you have now?

- How will you develop them if you want them?

_____

_____

_____

_____

_____

_____

_____

## A Compassionate Man

Moses was a compassionate man who cared about the dignity of his people. His early life's history is well known: He is placed in a basket on the Nile so that he might survive the killing of the Hebrews, and is found by an Egyptian princess. He is brought up in the court and is viewed as the brother of the next Pharaoh. At some point in his life he learns that he is really a Hebrew—a major adversity he must deal with because the Hebrews are enslaved by the Egyptians. He goes away to think about this new knowledge and returns to the royal court to make his powerful request: Let my people go.

The compassion is in Moses' determination to free the Hebrew people at enormous cost to everyone but with the desired objective of human freedom from tyranny. Moses is presented in the Bible story as a full human being. When he discovers his heritage, he reacts as a human would; he feels inadequate to taking on the task of freeing his people, he worries that he will not do the right thing, he seeks comfort. He is a human facing a major adversity and is not sure he is up to it. He needs help. God is his help.

The enemy is not the Pharaoh, whom Moses loves. The enemy is the system, the delusion that one man has the divine right to demand the complete obedience of all his subjects. Taking that system on was more than Moses wanted, but as a person who regarded others as valuable, he faced the mighty adversity. He was afraid and doubtful, but he persisted, with faith, in overcoming the adversities. He was heroic. He was resilient.

Think of a situation in which someone came to you needing help because they were facing an adversity they could not deal with alone. What was the situation? Ask yourself the following questions:

- What did the person ask for?

- How do you think he or she felt?

- What did you do in response?

- How did you feel?

- How was the situation resolved?

With that full description of the event in mind, now focus on the implications of the event for the development of your compassion for others.

- What did you do or say that helped you build your compassion?

- What did you do or say that prevented the building of your compassion for others?

- What would you do now if you were in the same situation?

_____

_____

_____

_____

_____

_____

_____

Now, think of an experience of adversity you had in which you needed someone to show compassion to you.

- What was the experience?

- What did you ask for?

- How did you feel?

- What did the other person do in response?

- How do you think he or she felt?

- How did the situation come out?

With that full description of the event in mind, now focus on the implications of the event for you.

- How did he or she show compassion to you?

- Would you have wanted a different way for the person to show you compassion?

- Would you have preferred fewer probing questions, fewer intrusions on your need to make your own decisions, or fewer invasions of your sense of privacy?

- How would you have handled the situation if the roles had been reversed?

_____

_____

_____

_____

_____

_____

_____

# 8

---

# Resilience in the
# Workplace

How many hours a day do you spend in the workplace with other people? Do they add up to more hours than you spend with your family? For many, the time away from home and in working relationships with others is greater than the time spent with the family. And if a good deal of commuting is involved, the separation time is even longer.

Now, if your workplace is a joy to you and you like the people you work for and with, then you are a very lucky person indeed. Most people report a great deal of stress regarding their job, with much of it coming from conflicts and annoyances with coworkers and supervisors. An amusing story I read about in the news recently had to do with two workers who came into conflict over how to arrange the names in a city directory that was to be placed in the lobby of a government building. One man finally hit the other man with a clipboard and a law suit resulted. Job stress was undoubtedly the cause.

## Stress

"I am so stressed out I can't think straight." "I am so stressed out I feel sick." These complaints are common. Some stress is good: It alerts you to adversity. It energizes you to take action. But there is a point at which the stress is too much and it begins to interfere with your thinking and health. You can't deal with any adversity in the most effective way possible when you have stress overload. Being stressed out becomes an adversity. Stress in the workplace is certainly an unwelcome adversity for many. Take a moment and identify the stresses in your workplace.

- What stresses do you experience on a daily basis?

- Do they interfere with your ability to deal with the inevitable adversities of the workplace?

- What do you do about them?

- Whom do you talk to?

- Is your organization interested in this issue?

- Are your colleagues interested in this issue?

The problem of stress in the workplace is so prevalent that many studies have been undertaken to examine its effects. One such study, from the National Institute for Occupational Safety and Health (NIOSH), a division of the U.S. Department of Health and Human Services, describes the prevalence of the problem of stress at work:

- One-fourth of employees in the country identify their jobs as the number-one stressor they live with.

- Three-fourths of workers believe the worker experiences more job stress now than was experienced a generation ago.

- Health complaints are more strongly associated with stress at work than with financial or family problems.

This is alarming. Fortunately, the promotion of resilience in the workplace can help. But first, here's a look at some specific stressors workers have identified. Which of these apply to your own experiences?

1. Heavy workload and/or long hours
   Are you expected to willingly accept more work than you feel comfortable with? This expectation is inevitably destructive to all concerned. The quality of your work cannot be maintained and the resentment that builds within you affects your sense of who you are and how you expect to be treated. Are you concerned about the amount of time you are expected to spend on the job? Some workers try to limit their hours to eight a day but feel pressured by their coworkers or bosses to stay late. Many companies offer

extra pay for overtime, but workers feel torn between the money incentive and their desire to go home, spend time with the family, and relax.

2. Infrequent breaks
   The workplace that does not recognize the need for sufficient breaks is not very interested in the physical or mental welfare of its workers. There are, of course, laws in this country concerning required breaks, but some work requires more than are allotted. Do you feel your employer gives you enough break time?

3. Routine tasks with little inherent meaning
   When your job fails to challenge you, teach you, or enlighten you, the work becomes mechanical and suffocating. People in such situations report that they feel like a machine.

4. Nonuse of skills
   The mismatch of jobs with workers' skills is often of little concern to employers. But you need to develop and use your skills in order to experience job satisfaction, and you probably feel demoralized when your talents are not recognized or used in any way.

5. Little sense of control
   The need to have some sense of control over your use of time and the demands of the job is important. Do you feel you are controlled or manipulated by others?

6. Lack of participation in decision making
   Do you need to get approval for every change you feel is important to improve the completion of your tasks? Do you feel you receive no respect from your supervisors or are you ignored when you make suggestions? If so, your self-esteem is being damaged.

7. Poor communication
   Many offices are physically organized so that workers are discouraged from interacting with one another. This separation of office space is more than an obstacle to productive communication, it prohibits a sense of group identity.

8. Lack of family-friendly policies
   People who want to take maternity leave or who need time off due to a family emergency are often treated with resentment or viewed as a nuisance. The Federal Family Leave Act does provide for such leave, however. Early in 1999, an employee with the Maryland State Police was granted $375,000 by a federal jury for compensatory damages related to emotional distress. He had been refused additional paid family leave after his wife had serious health

problems following the birth of their baby. Unfortunately, not long after the settlement he was barred from work and ordered to undergo psychiatric assessment to determine if he was fit for duty!

9. Poor social environment and lack of support or help from coworkers and supervisors

   Many companies are not aware of how important interpersonal relationships are to workers, especially when the job tasks aren't very attractive. Many employers fear that socializing on the job will decrease production, but actually the reverse is usually true—people work harder when they feel a camaraderie with one another. When I was a teenager I spent a summer working in my father's factory "to learn what hard work was all about." The work consisted of standing around a large table putting together boxes to contain the company's products. It was a miserable job and I detested it, except for the interactions with my coworkers. We had a great time sharing stories, experiences, and current problems with boyfriends and families. We joked together and even agreed to speed up our production line in order to take more time during our eating break. I was glad when the summer was over, but I kept in touch with many of the friends I made on the production line. When workers are isolated from each other, they have no sense of belonging or even being recognized as a person.

10. Conflicting or uncertain job expectations, or too much responsibility

    Many workers, and this is particularly true of employees who interact with the public, are caught in situations where they must deal with the rightful expectations of the customer and the limits set by the organization they work for. What does a worker do when he knows the quality of an item is not as high as it could be, yet he must respond to an angry customer without incriminating his employer?

11. Job insecurity and lack of opportunity for growth, advancement, or promotion

    Perhaps you've been with a company that has decided to reorganize its entire structure without letting its employers know where they will stand after the changes are made. This is a fairly common occurrence, as is merging and the inevitable downsizing that follows. A sense of insecurity, even incompetence, is sure to be roused in these situations. When workers are not prepared for the new job situation, they know they are vulnerable to being replaced, which leads to an atmosphere of fear and hostility.

12. Unpleasant or dangerous physical conditions
    Do you experience too much crowding, noise, or air pollution? Is your workspace unergonomic? The latter can be quite danger-ous—people suffer from back pain, muscle cramps, and carpal tunnel syndrome as a result.

How many of these twelve stressors affect you? Early signs of too much stress include headaches, sleep disturbances, difficulty in concentrating, short temper, upset stomach, job dissatisfaction, and low morale. Do you experience any of those symptoms?

Too much stress can even lead to serious health problems. Some demanding jobs increase the risk of cardiovascular disease. There also seems to be a connection between job stress and the risk for develop-ment of back- and upper-extremity musculoskeletal disorders. Psy-chological disorders are frequently seen: social workers and teachers often complain about depression and burnout. Finally, some studies report evidence of a relationship between high levels of work-related stress and suicide, cancer, ulcers, and impaired immune function. Workers under stress account for about 50 percent more in expendi-tures for health care than do others.

# Career Resilience

Understanding the role of resilience in the workplace helps you iden-tity the problems workers face and recognize them as adversities that need to be dealt with. If you have a job or a position in which you experience some of these adversities, you might engage in conversa-tions with others who have the same problems and work out possible solutions. You can use the "Suggestion Box" to submit ideas. (Your office doesn't have one? Then put it in place yourself!) You are not helpless. You are career resilient.

Career resilience is a relatively new concept that has emerged from the growing interest in employee welfare as well as a recogni-tion of the dramatic changes in career requirements. Career resilience incorporates the attributes of resilience you've been learning about: the availability of resources ("I have"), the inner strength of auton-omy, initiative, optimism, and persistence ("I am"), and the problem-solving and interpersonal skills ("I can") needed to address career-related issues. When you use these attributes in relation to your work, you are better able to deal with adversities that will inevitably emerge. You are not in a dependent position, relying on others to deal with your adversities. You are part of the solution.

Many people have spent a good deal of time determining the role of resilience in the workplace and in individual careers. One of the best reports I have read was made by researchers Robert H. Waterman, Jr., Judith A. Waterman, and Betsy A. Collard. They described the basic changes in thinking about the workforce that allows for the promotion of career resilience. The first basic shift was from the concept of employment to employability. The earlier concept of employment was developed when it was common for a company to offer lifetime employment. A worker was expected to offer, in return, good work performance and company loyalty. This view has lost ground to the more recent concept of employability, which, in light of today's downsizing, layoffs, restructuring, and merging, is more consistent with worker's needs. Employability suggests that the worker has acquired certain competitive skills and is prepared to find work as needed and wherever she wishes. The agreement with a company, then, becomes one in which the company offers opportunities for the worker to develop greater employability in exchange for a higher quality of productivity—with some degree of commitment to the company and its goals. Such a relationship is less parent/child and more adult/adult. Companies are no longer seen as authoritarian, demanding obedience and dispensing rewards and punishments at will. Do you see how this allows for the development of resilience factors from "I have," "I am," and "I can"?

When workers are seen as adults, there must be communication in which expressions of thoughts and feelings are respected and new ideas generated by workers are taken seriously. In effect, workers are being encouraged to be independent ("I have"), to plan for the future ("I am"), and to solve problems in various settings ("I can").

## Ingredients of Career Resilience

Career resilience includes a variety of ingredients that prepare the worker to make decisions about what she wants to do and where she wants to do it. The first ingredient is self-assessment.

Self-assessment has to do with determining your skills, interests, values, and temperament. If you know that you have a tendency to become impatient with unhappy, critical customers, you certainly do not want to put your energies into a job that requires you to deal with them. If you have certain ethical or moral beliefs that you feel strongly about, you know you don't want to work for a company that doesn't share those beliefs. If learning new things is important to you, you don't want to work in a place that is unable to add to your knowledge.

A general ignorance of who we are, what we feel, and how others perceive us continues to be a problem for many people. Such people are unaware of how their style of work affects others or how their interpersonal relationships influences how people react to them. Surprisingly, some people simply lack an awareness of which work-related skills or interests have the potential to excite and challenge them. Yet there are tests and resources available to address these gaps in information. Often, the human resources division takes the lead in providing these assessment tools. The tools may include a temperament test, tests of technical competence, an interest inventory, or a test of social and interpersonal skills. These tests are usually interpreted by a specialist and are useful for learning more about yourself and your talent. The results help you make decisions.

The second ingredient of career resilience is the acquisition of competitive skills. To develop the new skills you need or will need for another job, you need to be aware of the direction the company is taking, what future skills might be needed, and what's happening in the economic market specifically related to your career. You are more likely to stay with a company, contribute to its growth, and become better prepared for future roles if you are kept informed. Many companies are beginning to provide training in how to plan for the future. If your company is one of these, take advantage of what they have to offer ("I am an achiever who plans for the future").

The third ingredient of career resilience is being informed about job openings. The majority of companies today announce job openings within their organization and sometimes even jobs outside the company—a real change from the past. Some companies even provide funds for training employees in writing résumés and learning interviewing skills! And, increasingly, websites are used for posting positions, providing career advice, and making information about job openings available. Employers now realize that preparing someone who is already within the company is more fruitful than hiring someone from the outside. The person inside is already familiar with and accepted by the company culture, and should be able to take on new tasks and responsibilities from a more solid position.

## The "I Have," "I Am," "I Can" Paradigm and Career Resilience

### I Have One or More Persons I Can Trust

This is important in career resilience primarily because you need to know you have loving support behind your decisions as well as your experiences of adversity on the job. What can be more devastating than to have people at home against you as you try to deal with job stress? Perhaps there are people at work you can trust as well. Hopefully, your company has human resource centers that can be trusted to carry out company policies and public laws and provide assessment tools or training programs.

### I Have Limits to My Behavior

A genuine risk most companies have to deal with is the risk of being taken advantage of. In this regard it is important to recognize the limits of career resilience. Being self-reliant and goal-oriented does not mean you are free to do as you wish without working within the boundaries of company policy. Acquiring new skills and understanding oneself better does not mean that such growth is to be used to unfairly manipulate the company. Self-reliance does not exclude the need to recognize and respect limits of behavior the company can accept or tolerate.

### I Have People Who Encourage Me to Be Independent

Your company promotes your independence when it accepts career resilience as a process and as a goal. As discussed above, many companies are doing this by providing outside training such as workshops and seminars. Hopefully, your company appreciates independent thinking and your contribution of ideas for such things as company growth.

### I Have Good Role Models

Do you have friends or family members whose career path embodies all of the resilience factors discussed in this chapter? Talk with them about how they were able to place themselves in such a position. Did they use the resilience factors consciously?

### I Have Access to Health, Education, and the Social and Security Services I Need

Most companies now provide health coverage for dependents as well as employees. Most also provide counseling services for people with personal problems that affect their work. There are also laws that provide for family leave. In terms of safety and security, there are not only laws that require certain safety standards, but in many companies situated in risky neighborhoods, security personnel will accompany an individual to his or her car. Being in a safe environment is important to the promotion of career resilience.

### I Am a Person Most People Like

Have you ever noticed how employees tend to gather around one particular person for banter and humor? The person sets the tone by responding positively to what others say and by initiating many pleasant comments. Workers can become likable by being friendly, showing empathy and concern, helping out when needed without complaining, and helping fellow workers feel comfortable and appreciated.

### I Am Generally Calm and Good-Natured

Not overreacting to stress or unfair treatment is very important. You can learn to recognize your reactions to stress and use stress-reducing actions such as taking deep breaths, listening to calming music, or meditating.

### I Am an Achiever Who Plans for the Future

This one really gets to the heart of career resilience. Setting goals and organizing time and resources for achieving those goals is crucial to the promotion of career resilience. What skills do you need right now? Which will you need next year? In five years? What knowledge do you need? How do you go about turning your plans into successful actions?

### I Am a Person Who Respects Myself and Others

If you are going to become increasingly independent in the workforce, your character and attitudes toward others are important. When you respect others and their opinions, you also expect them to respect yours. Do you have a plan of action in place for respectfully dealing with very difficult people?

### I Am Empathic and Caring of Others

The concepts of empathy and altruism are embedded in the broader concept of compassionate interpersonal relationships. Of course, career resilience is enhanced by such feelings for others. Altruism is particularly important when you're working within a team.

### I Am Responsible for My Own Behavior and Accept the Consequences

Clearly, the increased independence needed for career resilience requires a greater sense of responsibility for decisions and actions. Blaming may reduce tension in the short term, but has negative ramifications. As a responsible employee, you must always ask yourself, What part of what happened is because of what I did?

### I Am a Confident, Optimistic, Hopeful Person

These qualities are extremely necessary in career resilience, because of the risks that go along with becoming increasingly independent, self-motivated, and responsible for decisions. For example, when you are making independent decisions at work, you need to have the confidence that they are good ones and won't lead to failure. When you assume more responsibility for what your career is going to look like in the near and long-term future, you need to be optimistic that you will be successful and fulfilled.

### I Can Generate New Ideas or New Ways to Do Things

Do you contribute new ideas or reorganize old methods or ways of thought at work? When you're looking for work, do you come to interviews prepared with ideas for the company? One of the great challenges in career resilience is the greater freedom that makes it possible to suggest new ideas. When a company or an organization encourages career resilience in its workers, it *expects* ideas to emerge. You have the opportunity—the challenge—to take the initiative in suggesting a new way to solve a problem.

### I Can Stay with a Task Until It Is Finished

Do you have a strong work ethic? Persistence is critical to career resilience. By being more independent, without clear limits of action being set by someone else, you may be tempted to put off completing tasks. Procrastination is easy to turn to when a task becomes boring, so this resilience factor is a skill that needs to be built. "I want to stop doing this task because I am bored with it. But it needs to be completed today so the team I am working with can put all the parts together tomorrow. I'll stick with it."

### I Can See the Humor in Life and Use It to Reduce Tensions

People with a good sense of humor break the tension and keep things in perspective when crises occur at work. Anytime work requires interactions with others in planning, teamwork, leadership, or critiquing, tensions and conflicts will arise. And there is nothing more useful in breaking tension than humor. Even when there are interpersonal conflicts, humor can diffuse the tensions so that those involved are not so uptight when they deal with the conflict. You may want to have some jokes or funny stories ready!

## I Can Express Thoughts and Feelings in Communication with Others

Do you need to organize your thoughts, recognize and express your feelings, and increase your conversational skills in the workplace? Many offices tend to develop hierarchical relationships, but there is greater freedom of expression of thoughts and feelings among equals than in a hierarchical relationship. Have you experimented with treating everyone in your office as an equal? When a group communicates well, it is in a better position to address the common adversities they experience as they carry out their tasks.

## I Can Solve Problems in Various Settings

The work setting is full of problems from a wide range of sources. Applying problem-solving skills to the inevitable problems will increase your career resilience. You will probably need to solve problems *with* others, so skill at team problem-solving is crucial. Can you do that without dominating the process? Can you do that without being critical of others? Can you compromise or negotiate solutions? Remember, problems can become adversities. The more you prevent that outcome, the more your resilience is working for you.

## I Can Manage My Behavior

Your increased responsibilities as a person who is developing career resilience includes managing your own behavior. No verbal (or physical, of course) attacks. No foul language. No whining. No blaming.

## I Can Reach Out for Help When I Need It

Knowing where resources are, who is available for help, and how you formulate questions to ask—all are required of someone interested in career resilience.

## *How Is Your Career Resilience?*

- Which of the three ingredients of career resilience discussed earlier do you have already?

- Which do you think you need?

- Which resilience factors need to be strengthened?

- Which are okay but can be built upon?

- What dynamic interaction of resilience factors would improve your career resilience?

- What plan of action do you have for becoming more career resilient?

- What can you think of that would help you be part of a resilient workforce? Can you lay out a plan? Here's an example of how to lay out a plan. Let's say you want to change jobs. You can see that the organization is planning to shift its attention from writing advertising to soliciting sale of products, and that doesn't interest you. Your new plan is going to be organized around the three ingredients of career resilience:

1. Self-assessment

    a. I am a good writer and sketcher; my ads are creative and attention-getting.

    b. I like brainstorming with others.

    c. I tend to lose interest quickly when I get writer's block.

    d. I have access to other organizations or I just might want to start my own company; I would like the independence to choose.

2. Acquiring competitive skills

    a. I will take some time to see where the field of advertising is going.

    b. Are there different styles of writing emerging, is the vocabulary changing, are my sketches on target for today's markets?

    c. Do I need to take a course to sharpen my skills?

3. Being informed about job openings

    a. I will do a search for a new position by examining newspapers, advertising magazines, and bulletin boards.

    b. I'll call some of my friends.

    I feel good about this plan because it uses the major parts of resilience: I have access to needed services; I am confident I will succeed in my plan; and I can acquire the skills and reach out for help when needed.

# 9

# Coping with Aging

The goal of every living thing is to reproduce. Many animals die immediately after reproducing. Many are ready to reproduce almost immediately after being born. Humans, too, are obsessed with reproduction, often in subtle ways. So much of our culture is centered around sex, and the concept of "sexy" tends to focus on those best able to reproduce: young, athletic, energetic people in their prime child-bearing years. This reproduction obsession has confused us. We think the reproductive years are the most important, so we fear aging and view it as a negative decline. The contributions of people in their postreproductive years are ignored; expectations for their creative work plummet. The young have ideas, the older don't. The young can take risks, the older can't. The young enjoy life, the older don't. The young will work, the older should take a "much deserved rest." Menopausal women have a particularly difficult time dealing with the changes that aging brings because they often feel that their value as a person has diminished. Unfortunately, this notion is played out in all forms of our media. It tells us we need to stay young, so we rush out for plastic surgery as soon as we see the slightest sign of aging. The message? If you want to succeed you must fight the adversity of age.

But the fact is, after the reproductive years are over, both men and women have another third or even another half of their life left.

What to do with that time? For the continued promotion and use of resilience throughout the course of your life, you should reexamine your life continually as you age—there is absolutely no reason to stop doing so at menopause or at any other time. No matter how old you are, ask yourself these three questions:

- Do I want to continue where I am?

- What changes interest me?

- Am I qualified for something else?

Reconsider old dreams you once had or new dreams you're just beginning to form. Do you want to work overseas for a while? Teach somebody something? Take violin lessons or learn some new technology skills? Think back—have you ever said, "I've always wanted to do that"? Well, maybe now is the time.

Find older friends or mentors whose successful aging can inspire your own changes. Talk to them about what they enjoy in life and how they made the inevitable changes that were required. Do they start new things? Have they, for example, moved to a new and more interesting place? Has their energy level changed? How do they deal with that?

Evaluate and modify, if necessary, your eating, exercise, and other health habits in light of your changing physical needs. Do some research to become knowledgeable about the changes accompanying aging—help is available in the form of books, websites, magazines, and classrooms. You will need to make a lot of decisions about what changes to make. There are, of course, health risks that accompany aging that will need to be recognized, and you'll need to seek advice and make choices that lead to longer, more vital life. Aches and pains or even the need for operations and medications can dominate life as aging progresses, but too many people withdraw and focus too much of their attention on their condition.

Be willing to let go of relationships, responsibilities, and old grudges and hurts that sap energy from your life rather than contribute to it. Sometimes you continue to assume responsibility for the behavior of a loved one. The fact is, that person is old enough to be responsible for his or her own behavior. Or, perhaps some of your friends expect more from you than you are willing to give—in fact, they may be exploiting you. Set some limits to expectations or drop the relationship. Finally, do you still hold any grudges? If you still hold a grudge against that person who took your job by some questionable strategy, you are the only one suffering now. Revenge is sweet, but if you can't do anything about it, let it go. It adds nothing to your life and, in fact, hurts it.

Reexamining your life—regardless of your exact age—can help you find new meanings that reflect an integration of past experiences with new goals and actions and give you the potential for new and rich experiences. Here are a few examples.

You can use your maturity and the strengths it provides to take on political, educational, and social issues—the adversities outside your more immediate concerns. Perhaps your children have moved out and you are now able to think beyond everyday demands on your time and attention to think in more altruistic ways about the larger good. As part of this larger framework, you can develop new networks to share ideas, plans, and strategies, and then compare results. You can be part of a formidable action group!

One way to do this is by seeking out younger people in need with the goal of becoming a mentor. You have years of experiences, with the knowledge that brings, to share with insecure people facing the adversities of life. Help them. You can help by seeking new career options for yourself: you can return to school, explore volunteer opportunities, or create new businesses or services. Help for yourself and others go hand in hand.

# Promoting Resilience While You Age

Again, the idea that aging gives new meaning to life is contrary to the messages put out by our media. But the truth is that aging provides a wealth of resilience-promoting behaviors. Here's a look at the resilience factors that deal with age-related issues.

## *I Have One or More Persons I Can Trust and Who Love Me without Reservation*

Aging increasingly involves the loss of loved ones. Your need for unconditional love and acceptance continues throughout life, however. As you age and experience losses, you need to find new people to love and who can love you. This could mean making new friends, but it could also mean reactivating old relationships. Begin to look around for such relationships so that you can continue throughout life to draw on this resilience factor. Are there nieces, nephews, or grandchildren you can begin to forge a strong bond with? You need to be able to reach out to such people, which requires you to be receptive to new experiences. Are you able to develop relationships that make these changes possible? Do you open up to others in a way that encourages them to become trusted listeners?

## I Have Limits to My Behavior

The limits to my behavior are set primarily by the physical limits I experience as the years go by. I do not run races, jump fences, or play hockey if my body can't handle it—I accept these limits. But my limits are not defined by social custom or tradition that tends to stereotype age as incompetence. My limits are to be examined against what is going on now in terms of my health and abilities.

## I Have People Who Encourage Me to Be Independent

Do you have people in your life who encourage and support your need to make your own choices as you age, even if your choices are untraditional in terms of what our society tends to expect from older individuals? You may find that, now that you've reached a certain age, others want to make choices for you. Do you recognize those who want to control you rather than encourage your independence and are you able to ignore them? Better yet, are you able to educate those people and help them see that you are skilled in making your own decisions? Your example will help them as *they* age!

## I Have Good Role Models

Seek out people who are dealing with aging, especially those who are well along in the process. You may find more role models than you expected. Of course, you will also find many people who are very bad role models. Between the two, note attitudes of pleasure or pain, optimism or pessimism, self-absorption or empathy and altruism, giving up or continuing to experience life. Frank Lloyd Wright is a good role model: he did some of his most creative architectural work between the ages of eighty and ninety-five. His humor throughout his life was astounding, and much of it was directed at himself. For example, he was in court as a witness and was asked by a lawyer about his occupation. His reply was, "I am the world's greatest architect." The lawyer commented that perhaps Mr. Wright was exaggerating a bit, to which the world's greatest architect replied, "Sir, I am under oath!" Here is a model of self-confidence, self-respect, creativity, industry, and humor. And John Glenn, as everyone knows, took a long ride straight up at the age of seventy-seven and stayed there for nine days. He is reported to have commented, "Old folks have ambitions and dreams too, like everybody else, and why don't they work for them? Why don't they go for it? Don't sit on a couch someplace, that's my attitude."

## I Have Access to Health, Education, and the Social and Security Services I Need

Here is where you need to focus a lot of attention as you age. You will need all the health services available, and fortunately there are great numbers of them. There are also universities that offer classes for older people so they can continue to grow intellectually and expand their range and depth of experiences. For example, Harvard has one of the best programs for older people in the country, in my opinion—it focuses on emotional intelligence. Imagine seventy-year-old engineers studying emotions in school for the first time! By learning more about their feelings and how to express them more easily, their capacity for resilience is being promoted.

## I Have a Stable Family and Community

As people move, as children leave, as relatives die, I can build new relationships so that I have a "family." Because I am part of a community, I can become more active in it, establishing relationships and contributing to its stability. Can I donate my time at a youth center? Could the hospital use my services? Can I help tutor students, be a mentor? There is so much I can do to help build a stable community.

## I Am a Person Most People Like

There are stereotypes of people becoming more irritable as the years go by, as well as the reverse: the elderly are often referred to as "sweet old ladies [or men]." It is important to be liked if you are going to be part of a community, part of a family. You need to be liked if you want help from others when you face a health crisis or an accident. Do you know if people see you as irritable or sweet?

## I Am Generally Calm and Good-Natured

As you age, you may find you are more easily upset and anxious because things are happening to you that you've never had to deal with before, such as your body reacting differently and your loved ones passing away. Just as when you were younger, you'll need to maintain and increase resilience by relaxing, thinking about the adversity, and examining alternative ways to deal with it. You'll want to think about your emotional reactions and your stress level, and learn to assess your feelings and decide how to deal with them. Do you need to take deep breaths? Do you need to take some time out? Do you need to express your feelings and then get on with the job of dealing with the adversity? Even if you never learned how to do these things previously, you can learn them now.

## I Am an Achiever Who Plans for the Future

This is just as true when you're older as it is when you're younger. What do you see yourself doing when you leave your present work? Will you train for a new job? Will you make a radical shift in your priorities? What do you need to know and do for any new venture? The more options you prepare for, the greater your chances for an exciting future. Most people are fully aware that they are going to live a long time. That is important. Thinking that you don't need to plan because you won't live long (perhaps your parents died young and you've convinced yourself the same will be true for you?) won't get you anywhere when the reverse turns out to be true!

## I Am a Person Who Respects Myself and Others

Too many people, as they get older, make comments such as, "I guess I'm getting old. I forgot to do that." "I can't do what I used to do. I'm getting old and decrepit." "I wish I had your looks. I'm getting so old and ugly." "Everything is falling apart. That's what old age is all about." These comments reveal a painful lack of self-respect. A person making such statements is likely to accept the same sentiments from others, all of which leads to not only a lack of self-respect but self-rejection and self-destruction. If you do not respect yourself, will anyone else respect you?

## I Am Empathic and Caring of Others

Here is where older people can excel. While children tend to be naturally empathic, boys are later encouraged to stop displaying that emotion—it is viewed as a feminine trait. But such pressures change as both men and women grow older and have had sufficient experiences of adversity, have built up sufficient feelings about dealing with them, and have increased their sensitivity to others' sufferings.

At a certain age, empathy from men seems to be socially acceptable again—and with more time they can increasingly transform that empathy into acts of altruism. Older people of both sexes can enrich their lives, contribute to the quality of community life, and help keep their own adversities in perspective by volunteering in hospitals, libraries, concert halls, schools, mentoring programs, and the like.

## I Am Responsible for My Own Behavior and Accept the Consequences

This may be a hard one for you to face. You want good health, of course, but what did you spend your youth doing? Eating too much. Drinking too much. Smoking too much. Neglecting to exercise. Now that you're older, perhaps it is difficult to face the long-term consequences of what you did all those years ago. If you are resilient, however, you have a sense of responsibility for what you did.

## I Am a Confident, Optimistic, Hopeful Person

This is a difficult resilience factor because the older you are, the more you've probably realized that many things do *not* come out okay. There is much suffering and tragedy; there are many overwhelming adversities in life. But we have the ability to defy such reality and possess a firm belief—no matter what has happened in the past—that things will, indeed, turn out okay. Many link this faith to God or to other spiritual aspects of life. Others have simply realized that pessimism and a lack of belief or faith leaves them in a helpless, hopeless condition that they cannot live with. Our minds have an incredible ability to reassess the reality of a situation and change the perspective so that the adversity is not so bad and there is hope.

## I Can Generate New Ideas or New Ways to Do Things

The rich experiences you've had as an older person can become the raw material for finding new ways to live, enjoy life, contribute to those around you, and find new meaning and new ways to engage in new missions—above all, to continue to promote resilience in creative ways. For example, one older man who had been a fine lawyer was tired of practicing law and decided to quit. But he heard about some youth in the neighborhood who were refused a place to play basketball by the school and the community because people were afraid the kids would create problems. The man turned to his former skills and began looking for laws that would make it necessary for the community to provide space. He found them in local laws relating to use of public parks. He made his case, with the youth attending hearings, and he was successful. His creativity not only brought a new sense of power to the youth, but several who were really impressed with the power of the lawyer to effect change decided to become lawyers themselves.

## Express Thoughts and Feelings in Communication with Others

There is an emotional intelligence in many older people that, generally speaking, does not exist in younger people. This is because they have had more years and more experiences with emotions—what rouses them, what ways they are expressed and communicated. Because they have had more experience with emotions, they can deal with them better. Older people are usually calmer than others in interpersonal relations. Some of this is because their bodies don't react as strongly (less testosterone?), but much of it is the confidence they develop simply from lots of experience. Do you find that you are less likely to become upset as easily as you used to?

## Solve Problems in Various Settings

It is a fact that older people have more trouble with certain tasks than younger folk: they often need more time to respond, have lost some spatial skills, and have more difficulty multitasking. Through some rather simple actions, these lost skills can be compensated for:

- Anticipate and rehearse solutions to spatial problems.

- Use devices to remember where you put things.

- Take your time and rehearse what you are going to do and say.

- Do test runs when you must go to a new place, or study the maps well.

- Take your time when you feel anxious.

- Involve others in solving your problem.

But older people have an advantage in that they have acquired wisdom. What is wisdom? It is a blending of knowledge and character and consists of expert knowledge about life. It also includes good judgment and advice about how to deal with the complex and unpredictable adversities of life. Wise people know about the complexities of human life and the various and often unexpected situations life presents. Wisdom also includes an expectation of empathy and a concern for the well-being of others as well as oneself.

Wisdom can be enhanced by being open to new experiences and engaging in discussion with others about the adversities of life. How have others faced, overcome, and been strengthened or transformed by experiences of adversity?

## Successful Aging

There are a few straightforward behaviors for maintaining high levels of functioning as you age: understanding how you react to stress, getting sufficient sleep, doing things one at a time, and being sure to draw on past experiences. Three specific actions that address ways to maintain high levels of functioning are selection, optimization, and compensation. The pianist Arthur Rubinstein is an example. He said he could maintain high levels of functioning as a world-class pianist by selecting fewer pieces (but those he liked best and was best at playing), optimizing his skills by practicing more often, and compensating for his losses by using variations and contrasts in speed to give the impression of faster playing. He was eighty years old when he said this—clearly, the adversities of aging can be resolved by using some tricks!

No matter what your age, the use of resilience factors right now will prepare you for aging.

# 10

---

# The Role of Your
# Cultural Beliefs

Cultural values, beliefs, and customs are learned. You began learning these things as soon as you were born. But what is learned can be unlearned; new learning can take place. However, changing beliefs and behaviors that were acquired early in life is a formidable task that fills many with fear and doubt. The cultures you experienced in the school, in the workplace, in the community, and in your home are deep-seated. Of these, the ones you learned at home are the most deep-seated of all. The culture of the family is tied to all our feelings and needs and tends to be accepted without question.

You need to be familiar with a range of different beliefs because they influence your interpersonal relationships, your expectations, and your ability to deal with adversities. When you are in the process of dealing with a particular adversity, you may need to know what to expect from someone with a different cultural background. Or perhaps someday you'll find yourself in a situation in which your cultural values are in conflict with the values of someone else and an adversity will be created. Knowing a few basic cultural variations and how they are expressed will be useful to you as you increase your skills of applying resilience to prevent a situation of adversity from developing. Preventing a potential adversity from happening in the first place is the best use of the resilience factors.

# Cultural Characteristics

The number of immigrants in this country has tripled since 1970. Estimates for the American population by 2005 project fifty million Hispanics, thirty-five million African Americans, and seven million Asians. Forty percent of Los Angeles already is Hispanic. Note that these groups are classified as "minority groups." Minority group status brings with it limited political and social power and the overpowering influence of the majority group. Members of these groups report that they feel not only a lack of caring about their needs but also that the values and behaviors of the majority group—Caucasians of European descent—are being forced upon them. Such inequity, disrespect for differences, denial of their heritage, and stereotyping is degrading and harmful to the welfare of the group as a whole. In terms of resilience, their particular ways of dealing with the adversities of life are misunderstood or ignored. The relatively new concept of "cultural competence" refers to the exploration of ways to recognize cultural differences in interacting with and providing services to members of minority groups.

Think about an experience you had with a member of a minority group that you found to be different than you would expect from members of your own group. Can you think of an experience that involved a conflict or a potential adversity?

- What was the experience?

- What in it pointed out cultural differences?

- How did you feel about it?

- How did the other person respond to your behavior?

- How did you resolve the differences?

I once had a problem while heading a unit that included a wide range of cultural backgrounds. I was having my first staff meeting and as I was clarifying my role, one of the staff, a Hispanic man, kept making caustic comments, challenging my authority, and laughing at what seemed to me to be inappropriate times. I said nothing about what he was doing and tried to deflect the hostile behavior. At the end of the meeting, I asked him to stay a minute. When we were alone, I said that I was no threat to him and wanted to work with him. I needed him in his position as head of one of the subunits of the division. He did not need to attack me verbally and challenge my authority. I was always willing to talk.

His response was totally unexpected. He said that I could have taken action against him because of his "insubordination," and that he respected me for not doing that. He said he would work with me, and he did. The cultural difference played out here was the reluctance of many males in the Hispanic culture to accept a female authority figure.

Another experience occurred in a Middle Eastern country. I was there on a semiformal basis and was interacting with some officials. I was walking in line with the men—all five of them. The leader of the group leaned over to me and suggested I walk behind the men, as was the custom for their women. Of course this was not an easy thing to accept. I did a quick assessment of the importance of my response for my sense of self versus a willingness to respect their culture. I had already accepted wearing a long kaftan. I didn't really want to accommodate any further. Finally, I said, "I don't think you can trust me behind you. I might trip you."

He looked at me in utter astonishment. Then, to his great credit, he began to laugh. He did not ask me again.

The international study on resilience I conducted gave me some useful information about cultural differences and similarities. The information is from countries in Asia (Thailand, Japan, Taiwan, and Vietnam), Latin America (Costa Rica, Panama, Chile, and Brazil), and Africa (Namibia, Sudan, South Africa, and Kenya). The overall finding from the research was pretty clear in that all cultures are concerned about children being able to face and overcome experiences of adversity. Each culture tries to prepare their children by providing loving support, being good role models for problem-solving, seeking help for their children when necessary, recognizing the child's need to be responsible for his or her own behavior, and enforcing rules. The differences between the cultures had to do with wide variations in age-related expectations, the encouragement of autonomy and independence in the children, and the degree to which punishment is viewed as something that strengthens children. Variations and differences also occurred in the resources available to draw on, the presence of hope and faith, the kinds of skills in communication, and the mastery of skills in problem-solving.

These issues are part of the study of cultural competence. Let's start with the major differences among cultures that have been identified in studies. These include:

- individualism versus collectivism,

- independence versus interdependence,

- separation versus family affiliation,

- acquisition for self versus generosity, and

- self-fulfillment versus interpersonal harmony.

Where are you on the continuum of each of these characteristics? To what degree do you feel your position on the continuum is the result of American culture? To what degree do you feel your position is the result of cultural values that come from your ethnic background?

In terms of child-rearing practices, additional interesting cultural differences were noted in my study. These include:

- pushing the rate of development versus letting it progress naturally,

- democratic versus authoritarian family,

- dependence versus independence,

- strict versus permissive,

- gender differences,

- cooperative versus competitive,

- physical versus verbal punishment, and

- free versus utilitarian use of time.

Our tendency is to see characteristics such as these as static and rather permanent within a culture. But actually they're changing all the time—sometimes quite slowly, other times with great speed. A study conducted in Singapore (Cheong 1996) examined the stability or flexibility of cultural characteristics. The study made comparisons with other neighboring cultural groups with the intent of identifying changes in traditional values of harmony, group orientation, and so on, toward more Western values of independence and competition. The results clearly showed that independence and competition were emerging as values, especially in the economic areas. From my own study, with data from Taiwan, Japan, Vietnam, and Thailand, I learned that educational competition occurs as early as the preschool level, where tutors are often hired to prepare the young children for an educational advantage when they enter school. This is a change from the past. Another study in Taiwan (Chia et al. 1997) indicated that Chinese are competitive and aggressive with outside groups but not with inside groups, where hierarchical relationships demand obedience and dependence. Cultures are not static, even though many of their characteristics continue to be identifiable. Changes seem to be made in cultural values when there are sufficient incentives or acceptable areas for change.

# Cultural Differences in Promoting Resilience in Children

There is, of course, a direct relationship between how children are raised and how much resilience is promoted in them. Children must learn to live within the constraints of their culture, which means that their ability to deal with the adversities of life are shaped and limited by their culture. But, again, no matter what the culture, some people are more or less resilient than others even though their backgrounds are the same. This does not mean that resilience is independent of culture. It means, rather, that resilience can be developed in a range of cultural settings and cultural characteristics. Here's a look at the nine major differences in cultural characteristics of child rearing (from the above list) and how resilience can be promoted in each case.

## Pushing the Rate of Development versus Letting It Progress Naturally

The speed with which development can be advanced is important to some cultures. This push for autonomy and independence is particularly common in different parts of the world with regard to girls. Often, they are toilet trained early, taught to become dexterous in handling food and household utensils, and trained to look after siblings. The girls are needed by their mothers to help around the house and so are pushed into the role quite early in comparison to other cultures. The result is the encouragement of early independence, which resilient girls use to take care of themselves in a not-always-friendly world. Their brothers are often not so burdened and have a more leisurely time in their development. Their resilience may come more from reaching out for help and developing good interpersonal relationships. In contrast, other cultures give children about six years of total freedom to grow before being thrust into the "real" world where self-control and discipline are introduced. American culture falls into this category; our schools are built on this model. Most children benefit from this model, but there are many, especially those who are shy and withdrawn or are not ready to deal with limits to their behavior, who cannot make it. These children become depressed, act out aggressively, or fail. There are different rates not only in growth but also in acquiring the basic building blocks of resilience. Unfortunately, there is not always sufficient accommodation for the latter.

## Democratic versus Authoritarian Family

This refers to the differences in how much the wishes or opinions of children are considered in family decisions. In an extremely authoritarian model, children will be given very little input even when the decision directly affects them, and the same is usually true for their mothers. This lack of democracy may well be countered by a great concern on the part of the parents that their children be well protected. The family may have a highly developed system (handed down generation after generation) of decision making for the benefit of the child. I remember bumping into this pattern of family decision making when I lived in Puerto Rico. I had a friend who was planning to go to medical school, and I asked him which one he would be attending. He replied that he didn't know because he was waiting for his relatives to hold a meeting to make that decision! In such a family, some of the resilience factors are very difficult to promote (such as independence) but others are particularly strong (family that is always there for you).

## Dependence versus Independence

Probably the most notable cultural difference in families is the degree to which family members are dependent or independent of other members. At what point can children make their own decisions? When can a family member decide on her own that she is going to take a certain job, go to a certain place, or solve her own problems? This is one of the most difficult adjustments families are faced with when they move to a place in which entirely different expectations are in place. In my resilience study, dependence versus independence was one of the most sensitive touchstones for determining cultural differences. I often found that girls were kept dependent longer than boys and rules were stricter for them. Girls and boys with different experiences in this regard deal with adversities differently—the more dependent the children, the more they relied on the parents to deal with the adversities. Parents who promote independence in their children tend to teach their children specific ways to deal with adversities: "Dial 911," "Call me at work," or "Go over to the neighbor if I am not home when you come from school."

## Strict versus Permissive

Setting limits for what a child can or cannot do and where a child can or cannot go varies among cultures. Sometimes limits are set only when it appears a child will injure himself or someone else. When strict limits of behavior are set, they provide security for children but they also rob them of an opportunity to explore new places and activities. As children try new things and explore new places, they build up experiences of bumps, spills, and problems and learn to deal with them, becoming more resilient in the process. When there are no limits—permissiveness is the rule—a child who is adventurous does not know when to stop and is very likely to get into dangerous situations. On the other hand, a shy child can be so intimidated by the freedom that he or she may well go off into a corner and play with one toy continuously. I found many, many examples of both these extremes in the international resilience research.

## Gender Differences

Unfortunately, in some cultures male dominance in all things, including "ownership" of the children, continues. Some cultures place a great deal of emphasis on the dominance of the man (first the father, then the son), in the family and in the larger society. Major cultural differences in the role of the father include the amount of time a father spends with his children, what kinds of activities they engage in, the degree of risk they encourage their children to take, and the differential treatment of the sons and daughters. In the many families where the absence of the father is common, he loses a great deal of his effectiveness in promoting the development of resilience in his children.

An important gender difference that cuts across cultures, however, involves the different ways men and women, boys and girls, deal with adversities. Even as both men and women reflect their cultural values, there are consistent patterns of gender differences in dealing with adversities. Women tend to use empathy, faith, interpersonal relationships, and family supports to deal with adversities. Men tend to be more pragmatic. They size up the adversity, make some decisions about consequences to specific actions they might take, and then act. They may or may not involve others. Boys as young as nine show this pattern and girls begin even younger than that to show the pattern more common in women.

## Cooperative versus Competitive

Cultures differ on which they tend to emphasize—cooperation or competition. Many studies indicate that Euro-Americans are competitive while Latino-Hispanics are cooperative. I have two experiences with this I recall that are qualifiers to such a statement. One involved my son. As a Euro-American, he was supposed to reflect this competitiveness. When he attended camp during the summer he was thirteen years old, he was greeted with a continuous agenda of competitive sports and competitive craft work. He was doing great on points won and his buddy at camp was also doing well, but not quite as well. So, Jim refused to win any more points until he and his friend could tie for first place. And that is what happened. When he reported this event back home, I was stunned. "Hey, kid," said I. "The game is to win!" "No," said he, "it was more fun sharing the prize with my friend. Besides, we each got one. And was the camp director ever shocked!" I was humbled.

The other story concerns research conducted on the West Coast comparing cooperative and competitive behavior among Euro-American and Latino-American school children. As the researchers predicted, the Euro-Americans were more competitive in problem-solving, while the Hispanics were more cooperative in problem-solving. I was the director of research for an agency at the time and had some supervisory responsibility for the research. It was difficult for me to accept such dichotomized findings, even though I under-stood the cultural characteristics. So I suggested they test their data by controlling for intelligence. I also offered a probable finding: the higher the intelligence of members of each group, the more the mem-bers of each group would shift back and forth from competition to cooperation as the respective solutions to the problems suggested would be helpful. Bingo! That is exactly what they found. Now, I respect and learn from cultural differences. But it might be that the cultural determination of behavior is not so rigid as assumed. These two stories are not intended to detract from our topic of important cultural differences. I've related them here as a caution—we should not always look for expected behavior because that can cause us to interact with people of different cultures in stereotypical ways.

## Physical versus Verbal Punishment

The role of discipline varies from culture to culture, with both the kinds of discipline practiced and the triggers for disciplinary responses. Disobeying a parent or lying to a parent (the worst offense in many cultures) often brings physical punishment. Other cultures place more emphasis on discipline through conversation: helping the child understand limits of behavior and why they exist, and then dis-cussing the consequences of violating the limits, and why. The role of discipline in promoting resilience is tied to helping the child become a moral and responsible person. Discipline is related to accepting lim-its to freedom and being willing to take the consequences of behavior.

When discipline is severe, however, the child tends to become fearful of bodily harm and becomes submissive, which is not conducive to learning how to deal with the adversities of life. When discipline is verbal, there is the opportunity to talk about what happened, why it happened, and what needs to be done to make things right again. Fear is not involved and so the child can learn how to be responsible without unnecessary anxiety.

### Free versus Utilitarian Use of Time

There are cultural differences in how parents view their children's use of time. Some cultures stress the importance of play and freedom of action for their children, while other stress the importance of time being directed to "useful" activities such as family chores or learning something related to future jobs and responsibilities. Children in the latter case are seen more as apprentices than free spirits, and miss out on exploring their environment and enjoying the fantasy and creativity that go along with that. There is a clear difference in attitude toward play that is dependent on the educational level of the parents. Parents with more education encourage play while parents with less education encourage the practical use of time. There are exceptions, of course, as was noted in the example of Asian families who hire tutors for their children at very early ages to be at a competitive advantage for school. The use of time is highly related to resilience factors, especially in terms of which ones will be emphasized. If the culture puts high value on preparing children for work, then resilience factors such as persistence, mastering skills, accepting limits, and being responsible for behavior are more important. But if the culture puts high value on giving children freedom to play and explore, then resilience factors such as initiative, independence, accepting consequences of behavior, and interpersonal and problem-solving skills will be emphasized more.

## Cultural Variations within the Resilience Factors

### I Have One or More Persons I Can Trust

It is difficult for members of many cultural groups to trust people from other cultural backgrounds, especially if the others have the authority. For example, many members of minority groups will not speak openly with a Euro-American doctor, social worker, or teacher because they distrust the other's motives. The "authority figure" needs to be sensitive to this anxiety and create an atmosphere of informality and comfort. He or she can do this by not sitting behind a desk or speaking in a specialized language. Creating a warm, receptive, and compassionate atmosphere is critical to promoting the resilience factor of trust and allows individuals to address the adversity in a successful, empowering way. In your interactions with people from different cultural backgrounds, how do you communicate that you are trustworthy? What do you do or say to assure them they can trust you to care about them and help them?

## I Have Limits to My Behavior

When you need help from someone, you will receive it more willingly if you know the limits of the services. In studies of members of minority cultures in America, it has been noted that often members do not know the limits of the services and expect—indeed, demand—more than is possible. The result, frequently, is that the client is annoyed and disappointed and the provider of the services feels somewhat exploited. Being aware of cultural differences can help both clients and providers become sensitive to these differences in expectation. For example, sometimes an entire family will want to attend a doctor's examination of a family member and are offended when asked to leave. The line for limits of services needs to be clearly drawn.

## I Have People Who Encourage Me to Be Independent

Many cultures encourage dependency, especially for children and women. One program I was involved in aimed to help young mothers become independent and not rely so heavily on their mothers to raise their children. The program was successful in that the grandmothers moved, found jobs, and developed new interests. But the young mothers then became dependent on the program staff for support and services! It seemed that dependency was such a powerful aspect of the culture that it would surface in spite of efforts on the part of outsiders to bring about change. Fortunately, the staff was persistent and began searching for other ways to help the mothers become more independent. Have you had an experience with a member of another cultural group that involved dependence/independence? Was the person too dependent on you? What did you do about it? Or, perhaps, were you surprised by how independent a member of another cultural group was?

## I Have Good Role Models

Who should be the role models for members of different cultural groups—people within their own group, or from outside their group? This is a critical question because too often role models come from television, and the media is notorious for stereotyping members of different groups. Also, the very number of Euro-Americans on television tends to make inevitable their dominance as role models. As minority groups become more aware of the loss of their cultural identity, they are identifying many of their own role models from within. Have you had an experience with someone from a different cultural background in which role models became an issue? How did you deal with it? Did you draw on the resilience factors of respecting others and showing empathy?

## I Have Access to Health, Education, and the Social and Security Services I Need

This is where the concept of cultural competence has made the greatest impact. After members of minority groups felt their special needs were not being respected or even noticed, a movement to incorporate cultural competence into services began. The issue is not to provide services in culturally predetermined ways, but rather to be sensitive to whatever cultural differences may be exhibited. If a woman is reluctant to undress for a male doctor, can he be replaced by a woman doctor? If a client communicates dependency, can the service provider help the client set some limits to that dependency while encouraging more independence? If the client is reluctant to involve the family in decisions, can the provider consult with them separately? The fact that minority groups are underrepresented in so many professions adds to the problem. What is your position on this? How does resilience figure into your position?

## I Am a Person Most People Like

Ideally, our interpersonal relationships are so dependent on how we feel about someone else and how that person relates to us that his or her cultural background becomes secondary or irrelevant. We don't feel that the differences will interfere with the relationship, and we can focus on what brings us together. Do you have friends from different cultural backgrounds who transcend their cultures? What do you notice in particular?

## I Am Generally Calm and Good-Natured

Temperament is universal, but the expressions of temperament may take different forms in different cultures. Are you able to read temperament in people from a different culture? How do you decide when to approach and when to stay away?

## I Am a Person Who Respects Myself and Others

The issue of self-respect is particularly important to many members of minority groups. A lack of respect from the majority group lowers their sense of self-worth, which is, of course, disastrous to the promotion resilience. No one can feel very competent to deal with adversities if there is little self-respect from others. Have you had an experience with a person from a different cultural background who was having a problem with self-respect? How did you handle it?

## I Am Empathic and Caring of Others

Cultural differences in empathy and caring are not very prominent, with the exception of the fact that many cultures promote a feeling of empathy in girls earlier than in boys, and the trait is expected more often in women than in men.

## I Am a Confident, Optimistic, Hopeful Person

For many people, the human spirit is linked with their relationship to and belief in God. Some cultures rely more heavily on spiritual sources and interventions for dealing with adversities than others. Have you had an experience with someone from another cultural background in which your beliefs about a hopeful future clashed? Were you able to understand each other's position?

## I Can Generate New Ideas or New Ways to Do Things

Creativity can be affected by cultural attitudes toward originality. Asian cultures, for example, have long been associated more with imitation than with originality. The more a culture places value on tradition, the less receptive it seems to be to innovation. The American culture, by contrast, places great value on originality and creativity and rewards these handsomely. The very resilience factors we are using may, indeed, be culturally determined!

## I Can Express Thoughts and Feelings in Communication with Others

Communication is too often a problem among people from different cultural groups. Many people do not know how to make adjustments in their communication when it is clear the other person does not understand. Impatience is often the response or, worse, a dismissal of the other person as not too bright. This is especially true of Americans whose only language is English. Speed of speech is the first major obstacle, and regional accents add to the problem. How do you deal with the obstacles of communication with people from a different culture? Are you able to express your feelings to them without using words?

## I Can Solve Problems in Various Settings

How people of different cultures solve problems is less a question of analytical methods than it is a simple question of the temperament of the people involved in the process. The similarity of logic across cultures was made clear at an international meeting I attended in Paris. A French gentleman was expounding with great logic on the parameters of a problem and its solution. He wound up by saying, "And that's Cartesian logic." A man from Peru asked to respond. He gave his views with basically the same logic and ended with, "And that's Inca logic." The entire audience laughed heartily. Now, logic is logic, but ways to solve problems vary. This is where resources and their uses are often determined by the culture. The degree to which a person is confident she can solve a problem and has mastered the skills needed for its resolution may be culturally determined. Have you had an experience that involved problem-solving with someone from a different culture? Were there conflicts in the way the problem was handled? How did you deal with these differences?

## I Can Reach Out for Help When I Need It

The willingness and the ability to reach out for help may also be culturally dependent in that members of some cultural groups insist that they will only seek help from family members. Many are reluctant to turn to outsiders and even avoid printed information that can help them! This limits help with adversities and reinforces dependence on family members. Have you had an experience where someone from a different culture expected you to provide help when you were in no position to do so, or really didn't want the responsibility? How did you handle it? Have you, from your cultural perspective, expected help from someone you reached out to and found resistance? How did you deal with that?

There are few extreme differences among cultures. The variations are more in degree than in absolutes. But in a world that becomes smaller every year and where intercultural contacts are increasing, it is important to become more familiar with the differences that do exist. Interest in resilience has become international and cross-cultural. As you become more aware of resilience and become more resilient yourself, you may want to note the role of resilience factors in those people you interact with from other cultures.

# PART THREE

Preparing for,
Living through, and
Learning from
Adversities

# 11

---

# Developing a
# Plan of Action

Many experiences of adversity will of course be completely unexpected and you'll have no time to prepare for them. Just the other morning at six my husband and I heard four consecutive explosions and light filled the entire area we could view. The noise was terrifying and all the lights went out in the neighborhood. We had no idea what had happened. We saw fifteen police cars out the window and saw that one of the intersecting streets was blocked off. We later learned that a car had hit a utility pole, shorting out the transformer and high power electrical line and causing the explosions. Although we were certainly not mentally prepared for this experience, we did have candles handy and were able to eat breakfast by candlelight.

Many people have difficulty living through an adversity without a great deal of damage to their sense of competence and worthiness. And most of us are so rushed in life that we do not take the time to reflect on past adversities in order to learn from them.

Resilience is not something that springs up by itself. It grows over time. The more you plan to draw on resilience factors to prepare for, live through, and learn from adversities, the more resilience will be applied and promoted. Here are two examples from my international research project that illustrate various stages of an experience of adversity. In the first example, changes were made after the preparation stage—during the "living through" stage. In the second example, changes were made after the experience had been learned from.

After nine-year-old Karen's parents divorced, Karen faced the adversity of being alone in a big city after school every day because her mother worked. The adversity hadn't been planned for, because no one anticipated how Karen would feel. "I had to stay at home alone after school and during vacations because my mother works. I didn't like being in the house alone, and I told my mother how scared I was. My mother told me that she wasn't happy about leaving me alone either. She worried a lot about it. My mother finally put me in a daycare program so I had somewhere to go after school and during vacations. I was happier and so was my mother because we both knew I was safe."

The changes were made as the negative aspects of the situation became clear. This is an important part of drawing on resilience factors to deal with adversities. You need to monitor events as they occur to decide if you are getting the results you want or if changes in strategy are needed.

Thirteen-year-old Andre faced a similar situation: "One day my mother didn't return after her work. My dad wasn't at home. Both my brother and I cried—we were afraid because she didn't call us and it was almost midnight. My mother finally returned and explained that she was in a terrible traffic jam and couldn't call. She said if such a thing occurred again we must call our relatives to pick us up or come over to stay with us. My mother felt very bad about scaring us so much, she was crying, too. At least we know what to do now."

Learning from adversities is an important benefit of going through them. But the best formula is to prepare for them in advance, live through them to the best of your abilities, and learn from them afterward.

## The Process

The sequence "prepare for, live through, and learn from" may be interrupted or experienced out of order, but ideally the three phases are always there for you to consider and reconsider. Here are some questions to ask yourself during each phase of the process to help you better face, overcome, and be strengthened by adversity.

## *Preparing For*

1. What is going to happen?
   Describe on paper or in your mind exactly what the adversity consists of or looks like. You'll be making a certain amount of guesswork here, but talking to other people who have been through such an adversity before will be very helpful for you.

2. Who will be affected by the upcoming adversity and how?
   If more than one person is involved, the views of each are important to incorporate in your description. Will more than one person be affected? Will an organization be affected? Will someone you love be affected? Few adversities are limited to one person or even to one place. They tend to impact many people and places.

3. What are the obstacles that need to be overcome to deal with the upcoming adversity?
   This will require some imagination. You and others will need to think through various scenarios, suggest decisions that might be made in response, and then play those decisions out in your minds. Write down the possible consequences of each decision.

4. Who needs to know what?
   Do you need to consider reaching out for help at this point? Do you need to alert other members of the family, the school, or the community about the upcoming adversity?

5. Who can provide help?
   A critical part of dealing with an adversity is in the "I have" resilience factors. "I have" is the support system that can help sustain you through the experience. During your preparation phase, it is very important to know what supports are available to you and others who will be affected.

6. What inner strengths do I and others need to draw on as the adversity is faced?
   The "I am" resilience factors are the inner strengths that provide confidence and a sense of responsibility for how the adversity will be dealt with. It is helpful to recognize in the other people involved what their inner strengths are that will help everyone get through it. If you don't know what their strengths are, ask them.

7. What skills do I and others need to use?
   The "I can" resilience factors provide actual how-to skills. When more than one person is involved in the upcoming adversity, you'll want to determine the problem-solving and interpersonal

skills of each person. Again, ask them what they see as their strengths in this department.

8. Which dynamics of resilience factors will be useful in dealing with the adversity?
   The dynamic interaction of resilience factors is critical and must be flexible enough to change as the adversity changes over time.

## Living Through

A major problem of living through an adversity is that it begins to have a life of its own. You may increasingly find yourself reacting to what is happening rather than being proactive, that is, trying to have some degree of control over what is happening. You will need to become a kind of monitor of the process as you live through the experience. Here are some questions you can ask that will help keep you focused as you monitor what is happening.

1. Where are things today?
   Do an assessment of the status of the adversity. Is any part of it over? Is something new emerging? What can you forget about now to focus on some new part of the adversity?

2. How are the people involved handling the situation?
   Who needs to be comforted? Who needs to be encouraged to believe you will all get through the experience? Does anyone need to calm down and rethink what is happening? Who needs to reassess what is happening, what they can do, and what can be expected to happen as a result?

3. What new actions need to be planned and taken?
   Does someone else need to be notified? Do some new plans need to be made? Can anything be done to help break the tension you are under? (Nice food, a visit away from the situation, a long nap, calling friends, going to a show?)
   The major advantage to being in the adversity is that usually you must do *something* . . . and action uses up some of that anxious energy so you aren't quite so stressed. Taking action also helps keep you from feeling completely helpless—a feeling that can be damaging to your sense of who you are. A challenge to your belief that you are an able person threatens you at a very fundamental level. Use that as a motivation to do something.

4. What resilience factors will you draw on as you live through the adversity?
   Will the supports you need change as the adversity continues? What are they? Who are they? Where are they? ("I have.") What is

going on inside you as this adversity continues? Do you continue to have confidence that you can handle this? Do you find you can show empathy and caring as the situation seems to get worse? Do you show respect for yourself and others when you encounter someone who should but does not help you? Are you pleasant when you ask for help or point out something that is terribly wrong and needs correction? ("I am.") Can you share your feelings as this experience continues so that you do not bottle them up too much? Can you ask for help without feeling humiliated? Can you process all the information you have as you live through the adversity so that the problem can be solved? ("I can.")

## Learning From

Don't underestimate the role of hindsight in adversities. We learn from our mistakes as well as from our successes.

1. What did you learn about the resilience factors? Are you using them for the best results?

2. What did you learn about your friends? Did you seek their help without taking advantage of them?

3. What did you learn about support services? Did you know where to get the services you needed?

4. What did you learn about yourself? Are you stronger, more confident, a better person? Do you have some new insights about yourself, your emotions, your interpersonal relationships?

Here is a true story, broken down into the process of dealing with an adversity, of a family that decided to move to another city. Look for the "planning for, living through, and learning from" sequence. Moving is one of the most unsettling experiences a family can have. Moving is perceived by most people to be an adversity.

## Preparing For

1. What is going to happen?
   The trigger for the need to prepare for an experience of adversity was the dissatisfaction of the father with his working conditions. Glenn, the father, was a professional scientist who conducted a good deal of research and was in a situation where his type of research was no longer given the funding he needed. He decided he could not stay in the organization, but because of the nature of

his work he could not stay in the geographic area, either. He would need to look in another city.

2. Who will be affected by the upcoming adversity and how?
   May, the wife and mother who worked as a lawyer, was affected, though not in a way that was too upsetting because she realized this might be a good time for her to join another firm. Ray, the ten-year-old son, was not bothered much either—the adventure of change was exciting to him. The loss of his basketball and soccer teammates was distressing but tolerable. Celeste, the daughter, was another matter. She burst into tears at the mention of a possible move and locked herself in her room, refusing to talk to anyone or come out. When she finally came out, she said she was furious with her parents for expecting her to leave her friends and her own room.

3. What are the obstacles that need to be overcome to deal with the upcoming adversity?
   In addition to the usual obstacles of finding a place to live, selling the current home, and arranging for a new school, this family also needed to assess the possibility of May's finding new work as a lawyer and help Celeste come to terms with the reality of the move.

4. Who needs to know what?
   Each member of the family needed to be fully informed of what was transpiring as time went on. The companies the parents were with needed to know when they were leaving. The coaches of the teams for the children needed to be informed, as well as, of course, other school officials.

5. Who can provide help?
   Help was provided by real estate agents in both towns and by extended family members who stayed with the children while the parents looked for housing and visited schools in the new community.

6. What inner strengths do I and others need to draw on as the adversity is faced?
   Each family member needed a sense of optimism about the changes and a sense of responsibility for being able to come to terms with the inevitable. Being empathic with Celeste's feelings was especially important.

7. What skills do I and others need to use?
   The parents were good at the skill of being achievers and planners for the future.

8. Which dynamics of resilience factors will be useful in dealing with the adversity?
   All of the "I can" factors came into play to make the contacts for the schools, the real estate agents, and a job for May.

## Living Through

This is the hard part. Things don't usually go the way they were planned and new stresses are frequently added. Let's see what happened as the family lived through the adversity.

1. Where are things today?
   May had been so afraid she would not find what she wanted that, after being offered a position by two different law firms, she chose one and began work within a week. The decision meant she would be staying in the other town, commuting home on weekends and staying in an apartment during the work week. Glenn found what he wanted too and was free to make the move at any time, but he decided to hold off on doing so until the children were finished with the school year.

2. How are the people involved handling the situation?
   Glenn had not counted on May taking a job so soon and was quite upset about this. The children were very upset by their mother's decision, but she came home every weekend, was available for visits during school vacations, and allowed the kids to phone her whenever they wanted. They accepted the decision.

3. What new actions need to be planned and taken?
   When the family did move and the children were placed in school, it soon became clear that the school did not meet their children's needs. The parents planned to make another school change in the fall. Meanwhile, May realized she did not like the position she had taken and changed jobs again. She still missed the contacts with people in other law firms, so she would need to take action to build those contacts. The children needed to make enough friends to carry them through the summer because they would change to another school again in the fall. They did this by joining community teams rather than school teams.

4. What resilience factors will you draw on as you live through the adversity?
   The family provided support for each other and they shared thoughts and feelings. They were confident and optimistic, and reached out for help when they needed it.

## Learning From

1. What did you learn about the resilience factors?
   The family learned that by drawing on their individual as well as collective strengths in terms of the resilience factors, they could get through something that seemed very hard at the outset.

2. What did you learn about your friends?
   The friends the family had in their first home were a source of support and comfort—they were available for help and stayed in touch after the family had left.

3. What did you learn about support services?
   When the first new school turned out to be wrong for the kid's needs, the family had faith that another school could provide what they were looking for. The services were there, just difficult to find at first.

4. What did you learn about yourself?
   They learned they could get through adversities as a family. They talked about all the experiences they had and what they did to deal with the challenges and problems of moving. They were a stronger family now. They also learned things individually: Glenn learned that he would not have to be so concerned in the future about the family's ability to weather adversities. He could trust their strength and resilience more; they could have moved earlier quite easily. May learned that she did not have to make such impulsive decisions but could take more time in making commitments. Celeste learned that she could make friends anywhere and did not have to fear change.

# Practice Makes Perfect

If you do not have many experiences of adversity, if they are far apart in time, or they are radically different in nature, you may not be as prepared as you need to be. There are two ways you can address this concern, both involving practice. One is to practice each resilience factor (and their dynamic interaction with each other) in your daily life. The other is to practice resilience responses to "what if?" situations.

## Practice Your Resilience Factors

Each resilience factor can be developed not only through experiences of adversity, but also by your consciously practicing each one (and combining them into dynamic interactions) in daily life. Here are some suggestions for specific ways you can practice.

### I Have One or More Persons I Can Trust

There is someone in my family I know I can turn to and trust during an adversity. But I will not take that person for granted. I will keep the relationship fresh and reinforce it by spending time with that person. I will also begin thinking about someone else in the family with whom I can build another trusting relationship, because the one I trust most now may move, become ill, or grow too old to help me. Who else can fill the bill?

Okay then, let me see who I now have outside the family I can trust completely. Do they live close by? Are they available to talk to and share thoughts and feelings with? Can they give me the support I need in most situations or only in some? Should I look for somebody else who can help me in different ways? Let me see, who else can I build such a trusting relationship with and how will I go about building it? I will look around at the people I know and decide who is most likely to give me such a relationship. I have to give trust in order to receive it. I'll take the risk and begin some casual conversation with the person I've selected, and see how the person responds. If the response is friendly enough to talk about something more personal, I'll suggest lunch or playing a game together. I'll try telling the person something even more personal and ask that it not be repeated so I can see if my confidence is respected.

### I Have Limits to My Behavior

Do I know how far I can go in asking for or expecting support from someone? Do I know how far I can go in becoming dependent on someone else to deal with the experiences of adversity I have? I may need to practice thinking about and setting limits for my own behavior as I seek supports. To use rules effectively in experiences of adversity, I'll need to think about their value and their limits. Breaking rules can often lead to unwanted outcomes. I'll use my intelligence to decide what the rules are for and how I can use them—or, at least, respect them—as I express my freedom.

### I Have People Who Encourage Me to Be Independent

Do the people I look to for support do things for me or do they encourage me to try to solve the adversity myself? I must not become overly dependent on others, so I need to practice thinking through how far I can take care of things myself. Then, I can think about how much support I need. I must become very conscious about my tendency to expect solutions from others. I know I don't like myself very much when I do that. Am I able to tell by people's reactions—body language, voice, and behavior—whether or not I am depending too much on them to solve problems? Do I feel comfortable asking them what I am doing that upsets them and asking for advice on how I can learn to deal with these problems on my own?

### I Have Good Role Models

Are the role models I am using still the ones I want or need? Do they guide me as I become more mature and have more experience? Have my interests and concerns in life changed sufficiently so that I need to find new role models? Where do I find new ones? In the news? In books? On screen? In history? Among my friends? Can a relative be a role model? Perhaps I should read about how someone else behaved in an adversity I once faced or am likely to face in the future. Also, what is it exactly that my role models are modeling that I like? Is it the way they dress? The way they treat others? The way they solve problems? I will list my role models on a piece of paper and think about why I want to model myself after them. Do I draw on everything they do and are, or only some things? Am I a role model for others? Who are they and what do I do that makes them want to use me as a role model? Do I model behaviors that help in dealing with adversities?

### I Have Access to Health, Education, and the Social and Security Services I Need

Are the health services I need and will need available? Do I need to find some additional ones? Is my favorite doctor moving or retiring? Do I feel as safe as I used to or do I need to find some greater security for my house and workplace? Do I know where to find the stores, libraries, educational centers, or other services I need or will need? For example, do I know how to select a college? A doctor? A car dealer? Can I find a police officer, a firefighter, an emergency vehicle, and a hospital even when I am under severe stress? If I am injured or ill, do I know how to describe what happened, how it happened, and what I think I need? I will take an inventory and plan ahead as my needs change. I will build a directory of services I think I may need, and practice what I will say when I am in need.

### I Am a Person Most People Like

Am I friendly enough? Do I make new friends easily? Do I show my acceptance of people I meet? Do I need to change any of the ways I communicate my liking of others? To practice, I will smile at people I work with and give a greeting, praise someone I interact with when they do a good job, and bring some humor to the lunch table or to a working group to help people feel relaxed.

### I Am Generally Calm and Good-Natured

Has my temperament changed without my noticing it? Am I more irritable than I used to be? Am I less patient with people? Do I find I cannot tolerate some of the people I could tolerate before? Do I need to reassess my reactions to people? Can I find better ways to protect myself from being upset by others? To practice, I will calm down before I go into a meeting where tensions may be high and I will try to create an atmosphere of calmness in a stressful situation.

### I Am an Achiever Who Plans for the Future

Do I think in terms of the future? Do I still make good plans that are consistent with where I want to be in the future? Do my plans need revision? Are they too unrealistic? Are they consistent with my talents and interests? Right now, I will sit down and write out a plan for achieving a goal I have in mind. I will identify the steps needed and the actions necessary to take each step, then I will daydream or fantasize about the future and identify some goals that will likely emerge.

### I Am a Person Who Respects Myself and Others

Do I let people take advantage of me? Do I become indifferent to people when they show no respect for me? Do I show respect for others? Have I become forgetful about showing my respect? What new ways have I found to show respect? If I am new to this skill, I'll need to practice showing respect before I can expect to receive it. To practice, I will make sure I give my full attention to someone who is speaking to me. I will make positive comments to someone I am talking to and couch the criticisms in language such as, "Have you thought of this approach to the problem?" I will set some limits on how people treat me.

### I Am Empathic and Caring of Others

Do I show that I empathize with a person's suffering and pain? Do I do nice things for people to show I care? Do I give them the help they need and express my concern? Am I, in short, a compassionate person? If I have trouble in these areas, I should practice by first finding empathic people in books or movies and thinking about the ways in which they show it. Then I can emulate them, in small ways at first, and gauge the response I receive.

## I Am Responsible for My Own Behavior and Accept the Consequences

Am I aware of what has happened and who is responsible? Do I find it hard to assume responsibility and easier to blame someone else? What have I done lately for which I was at fault but did not assume the responsibility? Do I need to reexamine my behavior more carefully so that I make more accurate assessments of responsibility? The first thing I have to do is recognize when an action I took was thoughtless, dangerous, cruel, or had an unwanted outcome. If I have trouble recognizing this, I'll need to ask people I trust for their assessment.

## I Am a Confident, Optimistic, Hopeful Person

Do I still feel that things will work out all right if I do my best to deal with them? Do I visualize positive outcomes? Even when situations are bleak, do I still have the faith that there will be a resolution I can live with? Can I renew my faith by participating more often in the things I believe in (prayer, church services, spiritual retreats)?

## I Can Generate New Ideas or New Ways to Do Things

Do I still get pleasure out of suggesting new ways to do things and solve problems? Am I willing to take risks by testing some new ideas? Do I need to reexamine how much I use the same methods for problem-solving—do I tend to go to the same people or look for the same solutions? Perhaps I should read more books in areas of interest to me and expand my knowledge and thinking about where my field is going. That way, I can see what might be possible to add to an area in the form of new ideas and actions.

## I Can Stay with a Task Until It Is Finished

Do I still have persistence, or do I give up more quickly than I used to? Perhaps I should practice making a commitment to a project and following it through to the end so that I can remember how good that makes me feel.

## I Can See the Humor in Life and Use It to Reduce Tensions

Do I find joy in life? Are there activities I stopped participating in that used to give me joy? If so, can I find time to do those things again? Do I make people laugh? Do I find time to be with people who need more laughter in their life? Are there things I'm too serious about? Can I get a fresh perspective on those things by taking a break from them or asking other people about them?

### I Can Express Thoughts and Feelings in Communication with Others

Am I able to express my thoughts and feelings without too much embarrassment or hesitation? Do I need to enlarge my vocabulary for describing emotions? Can I pick up the emotional tone of someone I am listening to? Can I help the person clarify his thoughts and feelings as he talks with me? I will practice what I am going to say to someone who has upset me so that I am calm and have the right words. I can build a vocabulary of words that describe my feelings so that when I express them to someone, they really convey what I am feeling.

### I Can Solve Problems in Various Settings

Am I skilled at helping others solve their problems without intruding on their privacy? Can I solve my own problems? Are there some skills I am lacking? Do I need to learn some new techniques? Am I good at resolving interpersonal conflicts? What are some of the latest techniques being used? Am I up to date? Do I understand the role of emotions in thinking and behaving and in problem-solving? Do I know and practice the six basic steps of problem-solving?

1. Identify the problem and describe it in words, to myself or to someone else.

2. Design, in my head, alternative solutions to the problem. I will want to compare my solutions with the person I am in conflict with.

3. Modify solutions as a result of discussions with the other person, or come up with a new solution.

4. Take action. Put the solution to the test.

5. Assess the outcome and compare it with the person I am in conflict with.

6. If it worked, add it to my problem-solving bag.

### I Can Manage My Behavior

What techniques am I using to manage my feelings? Do I rely on control or even repression of my feelings? Am I able to manage my feelings without acting out? What helps me express my thoughts and feelings without doing something impulsive and dangerous? How do I slow my reactions down? Perhaps I can practice counting to ten before acting on a feeling, or practice writing down all my feelings before I confront somebody about something I'm angry about. Do I need to practice reading body language? Can I tell by facial expressions and other body movements what mood a person is in? Am I in the habit of using it as a gauge to know when to approach someone and when to leave them alone?

### I Can Reach Out for Help When I Need It

Can I ask for help without feeling as though I am weak? Can I practice by asking for help with minor things (moving furniture or planning and cooking a dinner party) and gauging people's reactions until I can predict how they'll respond? If one attempt to reach out doesn't work, have I thought through other avenues? Have I tried using the phone book, calling someone for information, or asking someone who had a similar adversity?

## Practice Playing "What If?"

A very good way to think about resilience in action is to think about possible situations of adversity that could occur. What if they happened to you?

### What If . . .

You are called into the office of the head of the unit and told that your position is to be closed down as a result of a merger with another company. You have one month before you will need to leave the organization.

- What will you do?

- How will you feel?

- What are some of the experiences you should be prepared for as you seek a new position?

- Who will help you?

- With whom will you share your feelings?

- What will you do if money is an issue?

- What resilience factors will you draw on?

### What If . . .

Your significant other tells you she has found someone else. She will be leaving that day and has already packed her things. Regrets are expressed but the decision is final. There is no possibility of reconciliation.

- What would you do?

- What would you say?

- How would you feel?

- How will you dispose of her things?

- How will you deal with joint financial commitments?

- What will you tell your friends, your family?

- Whom would you turn to?

- How would you resolve the situation?

- What resilience factors would you draw on?

## What If . . .

You drive home and see that your house is on fire. You do not know if the fire department has been notified. You do not know if anyone is inside.

- What would you do? Would you be able to call the fire department without panicking? Could you shout into the house and resist the temptation to run inside?

- How would you feel?

- What are some of the questions you need to ask about insurance coverage, about repairs and replacements? Do you have a log of your valuables stored somewhere outside the house?

- Whom would you turn to?

- How could the situation be resolved?

- What resilience factors would you draw on?

## What if ? . . . A Personal Experience

I had an experience I did not handle well while working with some troubled youth. In hindsight and after years of studying resilience, I now ask myself, What if it happened today? How would I change it? Here's what happened:

I was working with some troubled fifteen-year-old boys in a group situation. In a scuffle between two boys, Bob hit Jerry hard enough to knock him down and make tears come to his eyes.

*What did you do?* I scolded Bob and asked him to apologize.

*How did you feel?* I felt angry that this happened, but I was a little bit afraid of Bob because he was pretty big.

*What did he do?* He refused to apologize and said Jerry deserved what he got.

*What happened then?* I told him if he refused to apologize then he had better go home and think over what happened. When he was ready to apologize, then he could return. I realized that this kind of act was not the wisest thing to do, but I was angry and wanted him out of there.

*How did it get resolved?* He left. But when I came out later to go to my car, five of his friends surrounded me. One said, "We don't like what you did to Bob." I felt a lot of fear, but thought I should not show it. Instead, I showed respect for them and their interest in the situation. So I responded, "Neither do I, but I didn't know what else to do. I asked him to make things right but he wouldn't do it. What would you suggest?" At that point, Bob walked up to us and made some angry comments. To my wonderment, his friends told him to shut up! They even told him he had to apologize to the boy next time they were together.

I handled the situation very badly when I sent Bob away and was just lucky enough to say the right thing when his friends showed up. I knew I had been wrong and was really searching for a better way to handle such a situation. His friends probably sensed I was sincere when I asked them what they would suggest. So what would I do differently (and in the framework of resilience) if the same situation happened today?

"Hey, Bob, what on earth is going on here? Have you hurt Jerry? Are you okay, Jerry? Do you need some help? Bob, let's help him up and let's sit him down on that chair. Now, what happened?"

Bob is still angry and does not say anything, but Jerry tells what happened. "I was trying to get my lunch out of my bag and hit Bob by accident with my elbow as I was pulling the sandwich out. Bob accused me of messin' with him and I said I wasn't and to get lost. Then he hit me."

Bob spoke up then. "He's always getting in my way. Every time I pass him, he's all elbows or all feet. I think he sticks them out on purpose so he can get to me."

I would say, "You both sound pretty angry and it seems like you just add to each other's anger. Maybe we could talk about what leads up to this and why you two happen to cross each other's path so frequently. Are you okay, Jerry, so that you can do that now, or should we wait until you both have calmed down? What do you think, Bob?"

The boys agree to meet with me later. "Fine," I say, "by then we'll all be calmer and can talk this through so we don't have this happen again. I like you both and don't want to see either of you having trouble with the other. Until we meet, would you like to think of ways you can resolve this kind of situation?"

By using this approach to resolve the problem, I would be applying the following resilience factors:

- I am a person who respects myself and others: I needed to show respect. Even though the boys were engaged in undesired actions, they needed to be respected as individuals.

- I can solve problems in interpersonal relationships.

- I can manage my own feelings and actions.

# 12

# When Disaster Strikes

I don't know of anyone who better illustrates resilience in adversity than the actor Christopher Reeve. As is well known, his horse fell during a jump and his spinal cord was injured, leaving him unable to move below his neck. Clearly, he has been transformed by his tragedy: he speaks all over the country on the topic of paralysis and has devoted his life to trying to help find a cure for spinal cord injuries. He has used the following resilience factors to deal with his adversity:

- I have one or more persons I can trust: Reeve's wife and children are devoted to him. They have not lost faith in his ability to deal with the adversity. He also has friends who seek him out and keep in touch with him no matter where he is.

- I have access to services: Reeve has been fortunate in having wonderful services available to him. Recognizing that not everyone is in this position, he is using his wealth to help others in this regard—he is even searching for a cure.

- I am empathic and caring of others: in his caring for himself and all the others with the same condition, he travels extensively, raising funds and educating the public.

- I can stay with a task until it is finished: Reeve has made a lifetime commitment to his chosen task and shows no inclination to stop. His is convinced there will be a cure and that he will walk again.

- I can see the humor in life: Reeve makes jokes about how expensive it is to be disabled in America. Remarkably, he seems always to be smiling.

- I can express thoughts and feelings: Reeve has no trouble communicating, even though he has an elaborate system in place from the doctors to permit it. He has mastered his use of the technology.

- I can solve problems: a good deal of Reeve's time is devoted to solving the daily problems he lives with and those related to his mission.

- I can reach out for help: during his speaking engagements, he routinely asks for everybody's help in finding a cure.

Most people in the world face some sort of disaster at some point in their life. It can happen in a second, as did Reeve's injury from falling off a horse. Or, it can build and continue, as with hurricanes, mud slides, or drought. When we read about such disasters, we send money, clothes, food, medicine, and letters of love and concern—we respond with empathy and altruism.

In Honduras and Nicaragua, Hurricane Mitch (1998) settled over the countries for days, killing countless people and creating a range of problems and tragedies for the survivors. Yet reports from the region pointed out how quickly the people began helping themselves. Because of the delays in receiving outside help, family members from other parts of the country brought supplies and food to their stricken relatives, many by walking. Teenagers got involved in the relief effort, too, carrying jugs of water on their heads. There is a deep pride in many people that makes them unwilling to see themselves as victims. They want to believe they are capable of dealing with the most severe conditions and experiences, and believing it makes it true. There's no need for pity. They are strong people who will survive. They are resilient.

There are no promises of immunity from experiencing a disaster or in being involved in some way. But by reading about the experiences of others you can prepare yourself somewhat, should the same thing happen to you. With that in mind, take a look at the stories of disasters in this chapter and as you read, think about everything you have learned about resilience.

As you become more resilient, you are better equipped to understand the impact of disaster, deal with it, help others deal with it, and maintain the hope, confidence, and faith that this disaster can be dealt with and the damage can be countered. Those survivors who are transformed by the experience often become leaders of services designed to help others who are going through similar traumas.

# The Oklahoma City Bombing

The Oklahoma City bombing of the Murrah Federal Building on April 19, 1995 brought a national response that continues to influence our lives. Not only were we as a nation stunned and traumatized by it, but we learned a great deal about responses to such a disasters. We learned our weak areas in responding and our need to attend to survivors in more effective ways.

People at the site of the bombing and all over the country wanted to help. They showed their concern by offering help to the rescuers, bringing flowers to the site, and offering food and drink to survivors. The urgency of the disaster brought outstanding teamwork so that the bureaucratic barriers were removed and quick, coordinated actions could be taken. The concern for the victims clearly overcame any obstacles to meeting the needs of those people. Everybody had a sense of mission.

# What Do You Tell the Children?

One response to such concerns came from the Institute for Mental Health Initiatives (IMHI), where I am a senior associate. A few of us got together and developed a booklet entitled *What Do You Tell the Children? How to Help Children Deal with Disasters.* Over thirty thousand copies of the booklet were distributed in Oklahoma. Here are the suggestions from that booklet, using the "I have, I am, I can" paradigm.

## I Have

- Express your love for the child, both verbally and physically, more often than usual. Raising the level of psychological and physical warmth within a home gives kids a sense of calmness. (I have one or more persons within my family I can trust and who love me without reservation.)

- Maintain normal routines and traditions. Retain a sense of stability and familiarity in the child's life. (I have a stable family and community.)

- Develop and discuss home safety rules and practice emergency procedures. (I have a stable family and community.)

- Tell the child about the people—police, firefighters, and the emergency rescue teams—who bring things under control. Explain that they are always there to help. (I have access to health, education, and the social and security services I need.)

- Be available to the children when they need to talk about the disaster. (I have one or more persons I can trust.)

- Read stories about disasters, including how people deal with them and who helps. (I have good role models.)

## I Am

- Explain that disasters are real. Explain why they happened, and what (if anything) can be done to prevent such catastrophes from recurring. Putting experiences into words gives kids a sense of control. (I am a confident, optimistic, hopeful person.)

- Emphasize that man-made disasters (such as bombings) are very wrong for anyone to be involved in, and that the people who cause them must be found and punished. Teach the child that people make mistakes and do harmful things, but that becoming violent or killing people is never acceptable. (I am responsible for my own behavior and accept the consequences.)

- Help the child understand that he or she is a good person who would never commit a destructive act—and certainly isn't responsible for the disaster. (I am a person who respects myself and others.)

- If prayer is part of your life, encourage the child to pray when he or she needs strength. If your family doesn't pray, putting aside quiet time for reflection can allow the child to sort out feelings. (I am a confident, optimistic, hopeful person.)

- Teach kids that expressing compassion for the victims of disaster and doing something to help them is a great way to feel confident and in control. A child can be transformed from victim to helper by writing letters to survivors or contributing to relief funds. (I am empathic and caring of others.)

## I Can

- Encourage the child to talk about his or her feelings. Supply words if the child has difficulty labeling feelings. If, for example, he or she exhibits rage toward an event or the forces that caused it, you could say, "You seem very, very angry." Listen closely, because emotions may be expressed indirectly. Remain patient and understanding. (I can express thoughts and feelings in communication with others.)

- Tell the child about your own feelings, but consider the child's age and maturity and don't overdo it. Be clear and consistent; contradictory messages can lead to misunderstandings and tensions. Make sure your words are supported by your own behavior. (I can express thoughts and feelings in communication with others.)

- Encourage the child to express reactions in creative ways, such as making a poster or writing a poem or song in honor of the victims. (I can express thoughts and feelings in communication with others.)

- Discuss the kinds of emotional reactions people have. Explain that it's all right to feel angry, but not to attack those who make you angry. (I can express thoughts and feelings in communication with others.)

- Talk to the child about growing up to become a person who will help others, such as a doctor, teacher, firefighter, or counselor. (I can stay with a task until it is finished.)

- Encourage the child to take action and to be involved in helping the victims. Help him or her make a card or send a personal gift. (I can solve problems in various settings.)

- Let the child see you taking action, too. (I can solve problems in various settings.)

## Adversity Abroad

How would you handle being detained, against your will and in another country? What resilience factors would you use to get through each day? Can you think about that possibility? The most fully documented report of what happens in detention centers was made in 1993 by Margaret McCallin of the International Catholic Child Bureau in Geneva, Switzerland. Her report concerned the psychosocial well-being of Vietnamese children in Hong Kong detention centers. Through observations and a series of interviews, she found the worst and the best in the ways those in the detention center dealt with their situation.

The interviews were conducted with children up to the age of adulthood because children were assumed to be at greater risk than the adults who were also at the detention centers. Here were the findings that were most damaging to the children and did not promote or sustain resilience:

1. A pervasive sense of loneliness
   This was particularly true of children, regardless of their age, who had no relative with them. These children craved affection, guidance, and help.

2. A deep sense of loss and abandonment
   Much of this resulted from the loss of a parent through death or remarriage.

3. Depression
   This was characterized by a profound lack of initiative and a sense of hopelessness. It was further demonstrated by a strong sense of passivity and powerlessness. A depressive inertia seemed to grip many of the children. This is adaptive in the situation of powerlessness and dependency these children faced, but it does not contribute positively in the long run.

4. Fear for personal safety
   Girls feared sexual assault and harassment. Boys feared bullying by older, more powerful males. Many children reported a strategy of invisibility, withdrawing into reading or studying or neutralizing their appearance through dress, posture, and behavior to appear younger. This way they hoped to avoid being noticed and therefore attacked by predatory elements within the camps.

5. Current stressors
   The main stressor was the separation from their families and the constant worrying about them. A stressor of almost equal intensity was their fear of violence. They were also affected by other daily concerns such as confinement within the detention center, lack of clothing, and monotonous and unappetizing food. Of greater concern, however, were those who reported no problems in the center at all, despite acknowledging their awareness of the existence of fights, riots, and violence against women in the camps.

6. Delays in screening
   The process for screening to determine if the detainees will be accepted to stay in Hong Kong or be sent back to Vietnam takes

years. A constant finding was that this time lag had the most negative impact on the children. Length of time at the center and age of child combined to heighten the negative impact of the experience. The longer the children are detained and the older they are, the more they lose interest in life.

## Evidence of Resilience

How can there be anything positive in such an experience? Surprisingly, many resilience factors *were* found that helped the children deal with their situation.

1. Hope
   Even though many of the children felt the future seemed hopeless, more that 90 percent had hopes of leading a normal life. The strength of the children, in spite of their experiences, is consistent with the human capacity for resilience.

2. Planning for the future
   Access to education is consistent with planning for a future. Not only was education available at the center, it was used. The unexpected finding was that girls took advantage of the opportunity more than boys. These girls earned higher average scores than girls and boys in Hong Kong, scoring two years above Hong Kong students in mean level of education. Such preparation for the future is consistent with hope and persistence. Why the boys were less interested in the opportunity was not clear.

3. Feeling in control
   This completely contradicts the reality of the situation, and yet 78 percent of the children said that others did not control their lives. This suggests that many of the children made adjustments in their thinking and believing in order to feel in control. They must have had certain small areas of behavior and experiences that allowed them to maintain a sense of control even when they described all the things that made them depressed and afraid. What may have been operating here, and I am only speculating, is that the children maintained a sense of their own identity in spite of all that happened.

How incredible that these children in detention demonstrated their resilience in spite of the grim, dangerous situation they lived in. How much more might have happened if those responsible for the welfare of the children had known how to add the promotion of resilience to their interactions? What might some of those actions have been?

1. Form groups of children, according to age, to encourage expression of feelings. (This could be done through conversations with those trained to listen and help—some of the people working in the detention centers are part of national and international organizations concerned about children.)

2. Help the children learn to calm themselves when they feel overly stressed and irritable. (A leader could show the children how to shake different parts of the body to relax and calm down, or breathing exercises could be taught.)

3. Encourage the children to talk about the adversities they perceive and to find solutions or, at least, resolution of feelings.

4. Help the children link up with a person who can provide affection and reassurance.

5. Encourage the children to seek friends to avoid feeling alone.

6. Offer challenging activities that use energy and stimulate interest. (The children could build a "house" with discarded packaging and crates. Or, the children could form teams to play games.)

7. Encourage the children to seek help and guidance. (The children who showed characteristics of resilience sought help from whatever staff was around.)

## Finding Meaning in Disasters

What gives meaning to life is almost always the basis for shaping what kind of mission someone is eager to undertake. Often, life's meaning is made clearer by a particular event, and from that emerges a mission plan. What kinds of things give meaning to most people? According to one study, the following seven items (in order of importance) provide meaning to most people: work, love and marriage, birth of children, independent pursuits (military service, travel abroad, personal accomplishments), tragic events (deaths, illnesses, accidents), marital separation or divorce (because these things are often dealt with by finding new relationships or attempts at reconciliation), and major purchases (home, car, boat).

We often feel we are being tested or punished by the dramatic, traumatic events that occur in life. They often have no immediate meaning: Someone we love is killed. Something we owned is destroyed. A job we loved is gone. An illness strikes out of nowhere. An accident happens, leaving us in a wheelchair. Why do these things happen? Why do they happen when they do, in the way they do? By working through these questions a meaning can begin to emerge, and then perhaps a new purpose for your life—a mission.

A friend wants to commit suicide because his back was broken in a skiing accident and sports had been what gave his life meaning. He sinks to the depths of despair, and when he can tolerate no more suffering, he feels the strong pull of survival. He called it a "white vision." He decides he will live. He will find a mission. He says to himself, "I'm a social guy. I love to talk to people. I'll become a talk show host on the radio." And so he does. His mission is to send hope and cheer to anyone who needs it. This is being transformed by tragedy through resilience.

Another young friend gave up living for more than a year—he stayed in bed in a mental hospital responding to no one. During this time he was fully aware of what was going on around him and he was appalled at how he and other patients were treated. There was dehumanizing talk about the patients, much of it right in front of them. At some point, my friend decided to get up and make sure anyone who works with people having emotional problems treats them with respect. He formed an organization to do just that, and spends his time traveling to look over mental health programs, offering advice on how to show respect to clients. He too found meaning in his life as well as a mission—a mission that incorporates empathy and acts of caring for others.

I was once on a talk show in which two women were reporting on their experiences with cancer and how they dealt with it. My role on the show was to identify resilience in their transformation from adversity to meaning and mission. Both women had severe conditions of cancer. One initially dealt with her condition by denying it existed until it was threatening her life. Then she acknowledged it as something she had to deal with and did everything according to medical orders. However, she noticed the medications were making her skin look a peculiar gray color and she did not like that. She had always been proud of her skin and she wanted it back! So, she found some plants in her yard, tested them in different combinations, and found one that brought the pink flush back. She noticed her joy in this victory and thought, I'll bet other women are having the same problem with their skin. And so a new business began. She markets her product now, traveling around the country with a companion to help her, and makes women feel better. She is happy with her mission. Not only did she find meaning in her recognition that appearance is important to one's sense of self, but she was able to think of others in an empathic and altruistic way to help them.

The second woman had a rare form of cancer and the doctors did not diagnose her accurately. She went to a few other doctors without a clear diagnosis and finally gave up on doctors altogether. Instead, she went to the library and began extensive research on her symptoms as they matched different forms of cancer. Then, she went back to one of the doctors and told him what she had and what needed to be done. Fortunately, they listened and her condition is under control. Her mission became setting up a web site directory of information about all different forms of cancer. She includes information on who the best doctors in the country are, what the best treatments are, and what the best literature is.

Each woman had a different way of discovering her mission. The first was stuck in the denial phase until she could manage her feelings and then she acted. The other was a problem-solver from the beginning and kept her attention focused on the problem, with a minimum of feeling. Each woman had good role models, loving support from families, social- and problem-solving skills, confidence, faith, and hope. These women were transformed by their experiences of adversity. They are resilient. The show had been titled "Invincible Women," but I pointed out (not on the show but afterward to the women) that they were not invincible. If they had been, they would not have had to deal with their feelings and behaviors as they faced the adversity. Invincibility connotes a kind of immunity. These are women who learned from their suffering and were transformed by it. That is what resilience is all about.

# What Is Your New Resilience Quotient Today?

Now that you've learned about the basic building blocks of resilience, and you've examined the role of resilience in the different aspects of your everyday life, this is probably a good time to test your Resilience Quotient again. You've examined many aspects of your life since starting this book, and you've also had ample opportunity to test out the effectiveness of using resilience factors to face, overcome, and be strengthened or even transformed by experiences of adversity. How are you doing today?

Read each of the following statements, and think about how much each one describes you. Then write down a number from 1 to 10, with 10 representing "describes me the most." Then add the score numbers for all twenty-one statements: that total is your resilience quotient today.

Resilience on _____ (fill in the date) = _____

### I Have

1. One or more persons within my family I can trust and who love me without reservation.

2. One or more persons outside my family I can trust without reservation.

3. Limits to my behavior.

4. People who encourage me to be independent.

5. Good role models.

6. Access to health, education, and the social and security services I need.

7. A stable family and community.

### I Am

1. A person most people like.

2. Generally calm and good-natured.

3. An achiever who plans for the future.

4. A person who respects myself and others.

5. Empathic and caring of others.

6. Responsible for my own behavior and accepting of the consequences.

7. A confident, optimistic, hopeful person.

### I Can

1. Generate new ideas or new ways to do things.

2. Stay with a task until it is finished.

3. See the humor in life and use it to reduce tensions.

4. Express thoughts and feelings in communication with others.

5. Solve problems in various settings—academic, job-related, personal, and social.

6. Manage my behavior—feelings, impulses, acting-out.

7. Reach out for help when I need it.

## A Final Note

There is an increasing tendency for people to believe that they need to deal with adversities quickly. But all major changes in life require a grieving process for what has been lost before you can move on. An example of the folly of ignoring the role of time in grieving over loss is the experience of a friend of mine who lost his wife. A year after the death, he apologized for still grieving over his loss. He said, "It would be great if I could be resilient, but I'm still in too much pain." That is a tragic view of his grieving, and reflects the speed with which we feel all adversities should be dealt with. Grieving takes time, and there is no fixed time or, indeed, fixed stages of recovering from grief. My friend is, indeed, resilient and is using his grief to perform a labor of love by putting together a collection of his wife's art.

# Resources

## Finding Information on Resilience

I hope your journey through this book will be only the beginning of a continuing quest to learn about ways to further strengthen your resilience as well as that of people you care about. Continuing this journey can be as easy as reading stories about resilient people in your daily newspaper, going to your local public library, or surfing the Internet. Each of these sources offers rich information on resilience.

### Newspapers

As you read about people who have overcome great adversities, ask yourself how you would handle the same problem. Once you make resilience a goal in your life, you will be surprised at the number of examples of resilience you will find in your newspaper or in the magazines you read.

### Your Local Library

Most libraries carry recently published books on resilience. More importantly, most carry out-of-print books that you won't be able to find in a bookstore. Other library resources you might want to inquire about include indexes to articles in magazines and newspapers. A reference librarian can help you use these resources to find information on resilience.

## The Internet

My two favorite book-ordering services are: **http://www.amazon.com** and **http://www.bn.com**. When I searched these sites using the word "resilience," I got eighty-nine titles from one and seventy-three from the other! Most were the same, of course, but each site had some titles that the other did not.

Through the Internet you can also check the holdings of many university and large public libraries throughout the United States or around the world. For example, you can search the holdings of the Library of Congress, which has the largest collection of books in the world, through the Internet: **http://www.lcweb.loc.gov/**. This will take you to the Library's home page. Once there, click on "search the catalog." Then, after the new screen appears, select "word search" and click on "simple name/title search." This will generate a new screen where you can type in "resilience."

The drawback in doing a search for titles on resilience held by the Library of Congress or any other large library is that in the catalogs of these libraries, "resilience" covers a lot more than ways humans handle adversity. The term also refers to the "bounce" in floor coverings, the ruggedness of electrical circuits, and simply the everyday use of the term to mean the resilience of the economy or some other facet of daily life. Because of the varied uses of the term, you will get a number of false hits when you search most sites. Librarians get around this problem by assigning key words to books. The Library of Congress, for example, uses several key words for identifying books dealing with resilience. In my search, I found the following key words to be helpful: Resilience (personality trait): thirty-one items. Resilience (personality trait) in adolescence: two items. Resilience (personality trait) in children: eleven items. Resilience (psychology): one item.

If you aren't sure how to connect to the Library of Congress or any other remote library, your local librarians may be able to help you. Also, if you find interesting titles and discover your library doesn't have them, don't despair because your library may be able to get it for you through the Inter-Library Loan Service.

### ResilienceNet

The amount of information available on various web sites is almost overwhelming. In my opinion, the best place to start any search for information on resilience on the Internet is ResilienceNet, maintained by the Clearinghouse on Elementary and Early Childhood Education at the University of Illinois. The address is: **http://www.resilnet.uiuc.edu**.

ResilienceNet is designed to provide one-point access to all current, significant information about human resilience. ResilienceNet brings together in one source information about resilience from a number of websites, journal articles, books, and other publications. Depending on what your interest is, you will want to go to certain sections of this site. For example, the section on bibliographies provides lists of titles and related information about articles, research reports, chapters, and books included in national educational, medical, psychological, and sociological databases. But you don't have to wade through long lists of references. The folks at the University of Illinois have divided the references into subsections dealing with different aspects of resilience. You can, for example, look only for "guides and teaching materials" or, if you prefer, for items on "program and project descriptions." Other bibliographies cover "research and evaluative reports" and "general and theoretical discussions and position papers."

Perhaps the greatest value of ResilienceNet is the links it provides to other web sites with information about resilience. It does not supply links to just anything—all the sites listed have been carefully reviewed and selected by an international panel of experts. You can be assured that the information contained in each site is trustworthy and creditable.

Another unique section of ResilienceNet is its virtual library. This is a collection of full-text publications related to the resilience of children, youth, and families. Availability in full-text means you can read the article or report in its entirety and, if you like, print out a copy to read. Most of the publications in the virtual library are accessible directly from ResilienceNet; a few consist of links to publications on other sites.

ResilienceNet also provides a list of literature reviews; each provides a summary of what is known on a certain aspect of resilience. These reviews are written by leading national experts on resilience. Finally, the site also gives anyone the opportunity to discuss resilience-related topics and issues with others interested people. This is done through an on-site discussion group. Instructions are provided for joining or subscribing to the discussion list. Once you sign up, you can ask questions, offer comments, and read what others have contributed.

# References and Suggested Reading

Baltes, P., and M. Baltes. 1998. Savoir vivre in old age. *National Forum* 78.

Baruch, R., S. Stutman, E. Grotberg, and C. Auerbach. 1991. The RETHINK Method. Washington, D.C.: The Institute for Mental Health Initiatives.

Baruch, R., S. Stutman, and E. Grotberg. 1995. What do you tell the children? Washington, D.C.: Institute for Mental Health Initiatives.

Baum, S. and R. Stewart. 1990. Sources of meaning through the life span. *Psychological Reports* 67, no. 1:3–14.

Cheong, A. 1996. A study of collectivism/individualism among Singapore teachers. In E. Miao, ed. Proceedings of the 53rd Annual Convention, International Council of Psychologists. Taiwan: General Innovation Service. 315–330.

Chia, R., T. Lytle, C. Borshiung, and C. Jen. 1997. Differences in source and modes of locus of control for Chinese and Americans. In B. Bain, et al., eds. Proceedings of the 54th Annual Convention,

International Council of Psychologists. Edmonton: ICP Press. 67–72.

Cyr, D. 1998. How to manage your doctor. *U.S. Airways Attache.* (June): 40–43.

Erikson, E. 1985. *Childhood and society.* New York: Norton.

Garmezy, N. 1987. Stress, competence, and development. *American Journal of Orthopsychiatry* 57, no. 2:159–174.

Goetzel, R., D. Anderson, R. Whitmer, R. Ozminkowski, R. Dunn, and J. Wasserman. 1998. The relationship between modifiable health risks and health care expenditures. *Journal of Occupational and Environmental Medicine* 40, no. 10.

Grotberg, E. 1995. A guide to promoting resilience in children. The Hague: The Bernard van Leer Foundation.

———. 1997. The International Resilience Project. In B. Bain, et al., eds. Proceedings of the 54th Annual Convention, International Council of Psychologists. Edmonton: ICP Press. 118–128.

Keller, J. and K. McDade. 1997. Cultural diversity and help-seeking behavior. *Journal of Multicultural Social Work* 5:63–78

McCallin, M. 1993. Living in detention. Geneva: International Catholic Child Bureau.

Piaget, J. 1952. *The origins of intelligence in children.* New York: International Universities Press.

Rutter, M. 1991. Some conceptual considerations. Presented at the Fostering Resilience Conference. Washington, D.C.: Institute for Mental Health Initiatives.

Sauter, S., L. Murphy, and J. Hurrell. 1990. Prevention of work-related psychological disorders. *American Psychologist* 45, no. 10:1146–1158.

Seligman, M. 1995. *The optimistic child.* New York: Simon and Schuster.

Vanistendael, L. 1996. Growth in the muddle of life. 2d ed. Geneva: International Catholic Child Bureau.

Waterman, R., J. Waterman, and B. Collard. 1994. Toward a career resilient workforce. *Harvard Business Review* 87–95.

Werner, E. 1994. Risk, resilience, and recovery. *Development and Psychopathology* 5:503–515.

# More New Harbinger Titles

## MAKING HOPE HAPPEN

Shows you how to break old self-defeating habits, learn new ways of thinking about yourself, and develop the willpower to say "Yes, I can" and the "waypower" to overcome roadblocks and find new routes to your goals.   *Item HOPE $14.95*

## PRACTICAL DREAMING

Explains how dream language works, describes techniques to help remember dreams and ask them for guidance, and provides a step-by-step method to help you interpret a dream's symbols and relate the dream to your waking life.   *Item  DRMG $12.95*

## CLAIMING YOUR CREATIVE SELF

The inspiring stories of thirteen women who were able to keep in touch with their own creative spirit open the door to new definitions of creativity and to the kind of transforming ideas that can change your life.   *Item CYCS $15.95*

## SIX KEYS TO CREATING THE LIFE YOU DESIRE

Why is the road to satisfaction so difficult to find? This book helps you recognize your core issues and take the steps you need to take to create the life you really desire.   *Item KEY6 $19.95*

## WANTING WHAT YOU HAVE

Shows how proven cognitive therapy principles can hyelp make it possible to achieve contentment and meet the challenges of modern life with balance and serenity.   *Item WANT $18.95*

**Call toll-free 1-800-748-6273** to order. Have your Visa or Mastercard number ready. Or send a check for the titles you want to New Harbinger Publications, 5674 Shattuck Avenue, Oakland, CA 94609. Include $3.80 for the first book and 75¢ for each additional book to cover shipping and handling. (California residents please include appropriate sales tax.) Allow four to six weeks for delivery.

*Prices subject to change without notice.*

# Some Other New Harbinger Self-Help Titles

*The Self-Esteem Companion*, $10.95
*The Gay and Lesbian Self-Esteem Book*, $13.95
*Making the Big Move*, $13.95
*How to Survive and Thrive in an Empty Nest*, $13.95
*Living Well with a Hidden Disability*, $15.95
*Overcoming Repetitive Motion Injuries the Rossiter Way*, $15.95
*What to Tell the Kids About Your Divorce*, $13.95
*The Divorce Book, Second Edition*, $15.95
*Claiming Your Creative Self: True Stories from the Everyday Lives of Women*, $15.95
*Six Keys to Creating the Life You Desire*, $19.95
*Taking Control of TMJ*, $13.95
*What You Need to Know About Alzheimer's*, $15.95
*Winning Against Relapse: A Workbook of Action Plans for Recurring Health and Emotional Problems*, $14.95
*Facing 30: Women Talk About Constructing a Real Life and Other Scary Rites of Passage*, $12.95
*The Worry Control Workbook*, $15.95
*Wanting What You Have: A Self-Discovery Workbook*, $18.95
*When Perfect Isn't Good Enough: Strategies for Coping with Perfectionism*, $13.95
*Earning Your Own Respect: A Handbook of Personal Responsibility*, $12.95
*High on Stress: A Woman's Guide to Optimizing the Stress in Her Life*, $13.95
*Infidelity: A Survival Guide*, $13.95
*Stop Walking on Eggshells*, $14.95
*Consumer's Guide to Psychiatric Drugs*, $16.95
*The Fibromyalgia Advocate: Getting the Support You Need to Cope with Fibromyalgia and Myofascial Pain*, $18.95
*Healing Fear: New Approaches to Overcoming Anxiety*, $16.95
*Working Anger: Preventing and Resolving Conflict on the Job*, $12.95
*Sex Smart: How Your Childhood Shaped Your Sexual Life and What to Do About It*, $14.95
*You Can Free Yourself From Alcohol & Drugs*, $13.95
*Amongst Ourselves: A Self-Help Guide to Living with Dissociative Identity Disorder*, $14.95
*Healthy Living with Diabetes*, $13.95
*Dr. Carl Robinson's Basic Baby Care*, $10.95
*Better Boundries: Owning and Treasuring Your Life*, $13.95
*Goodbye Good Girl*, $12.95
*Fibromyalgia & Chronic Myofascial Pain Syndrome*, $19.95
*The Depression Workbook: Living With Depression and Manic Depression*, $17.95
*Self-Esteem, Second Edition*, $13.95
*Angry All the Time: An Emergency Guide to Anger Control*, $12.95
*When Anger Hurts*, $13.95
*Perimenopause*, $16.95
*The Relaxation & Stress Reduction Workbook, Fourth Edition*, $17.95
*The Anxiety & Phobia Workbook, Second Edition*, $18.95
*I Can't Get Over It, A Handbook for Trauma Survivors, Second Edition*, $16.95
*Messages: The Communication Skills Workbook, Second Edition*, $15.95
*Thoughts & Feelings, Second Edition*, $18.95
*Depression: How It Happens, How It's Healed*, $14.95
*The Deadly Diet, Second Edition*, $14.95
*The Power of Two*, $15.95
*Living Without Depression & Manic Depression: A Workbook for Maintaining Mood Stability*, $18.95
*Couple Skills: Making Your Relationship Work*, $14.95
*Hypnosis for Change: A Manual of Proven Techniques, Third Edition*, $15.95
*Letting Go of Anger: The 10 Most Common Anger Styles and What to Do About Them*, $12.95
*Infidelity: A Survival Guide*, $13.95
*When Anger Hurts Your Kids*, $12.95
*Don't Take It Personally*, $12.95
*The Addiction Workbook*, $17.95
*It's Not OK Anymore*, $13.95
*Beyond Grief: A Guide for Recovering from the Death of a Loved One*, $14.95
*The Chemotherapy & Radiation Survival Guide, Second Edition*, $14.95
*An End to Panic: Breakthrough Techniques for Overcoming Panic Disorder, Second Edition*, $18.95
*Dying of Embarrassment: Help for Social Anxiety and Social Phobia*, $13.95
*The Endometriosis Survival Guide*, $13.95
*Grief's Courageous Journey*, $12.95
*Flying Without Fear*, $13.95
*Stepfamily Realities*, $14.95
*Coping With Schizophrenia: A Guide For Families*, $15.95
*Conquering Carpal Tunnel Syndrome and Other Repetitive Strain Injuries*, $17.95
*The Three Minute Meditator, Third Edition*, $13.95
*The Chronic Pain Control Workbook, Second Edition*, $17.95
*The Power of Focusing*, $12.95
*Living Without Procrastination*, $12.95
*Kid Cooperation: How to Stop Yelling, Nagging & Pleading and Get Kids to Cooperate*, $13.95

Call **toll free, 1-800-748-6273,** or log on to our online bookstore at **www.newharbinger.com** to order. Have your Visa or Mastercard number ready. Or send a check for the titles you want to New Harbinger Publications, Inc., 5674 Shattuck Ave., Oakland, CA 94609. Include $3.80 for the first book and 75¢ for each additional book, to cover shipping and handling. (California residents please include appropriate sales tax.) Allow two to five weeks for delivery.

*Prices subject to change without notice.*